Design & Sew it Yourself

A WORKBOOK for CREATIVE CLOTHING

by, Lois Ericson

& Diane Ericson Frode

ILLUSTRATIONS & BOOK DESIGN BY DIANE ERICSON FRODE

Combinations, forms, and ———
juxtapositions of materials are
limited only by the minds eye
and what it sees. If you
actively explore the following
techniques, you will find yourself: • exploring materials more
confidently

• understanding more
thoroughly the design
process and working
with materials

• feeling good about what
you make and most of
all... having a good time.

The more you manipulate and
explore materials, the more you
will understand how they work
together.

— much joy in the making!

"Design & Sew It Yourself"
Revised Edition of
"Design It Yourself" 1980
"Sewing It Yourself" 1980

Copyright © 1983

Diane Ericson Frode
Lois Ericson

ISBN 0-911985-00-X

Contents

PART I

Desiring

DEFINITIONS....

Designer:	One who devises or executes designs; one who creates forms, and patterns; a plotter, an intriguer, a schemer
Create:	Make, originate, to cause to bring into existence
Panache:	Style, verve, flamboyant manner
Relationship:	A connection, tie, correlation, relevance, an association or involvement

SEEING

Seeing is a complex activity. Unlike looking, seeing is a skill to be learned; it can be acquired with practice. The more time you spend actively involved in this creative phase, the easier it will be to translate your ideas.

What are you seeing?

> Contrasts/Relationships
> Texture
> Shapes
> Color
> Line

Try seeing something for what it is.....not for what it's called.

Taking out of context, makes it new and vital...accessible again. The exercises below are important ones to practice. When these concepts become a natural or automatic part of your creative process, you will find it becomes increasingly easy to design something different and entirely 'yours'.

= Exercises =

#1 Sketching ——→
Look at a photo of a garment on a model for 30 seconds. Close the book, magazine or newspaper and record as much of the detail as you can remember.

#2 Contour Line

In relation to seeing and becoming more aware of what things really are, an introduction to contour drawing is in order. A contour is an edge as you perceive it, so drawing using this method involves keen observation of the object and recording what your eye sees without looking at your paper. This is not meant to be a finished drawing, it is a record of ideas for you. It is important to record your perceptions in as many ways as you can, i.e. sketching, writing, possibly include your feelings at the time, in relation to the object.

what you'll need:

- Object (from nature, household or ?)
- Paper (a sketch pad is a good record for easy reference)
- Felt pen or pencil
- Quiet place with uninterrupted time

realistic

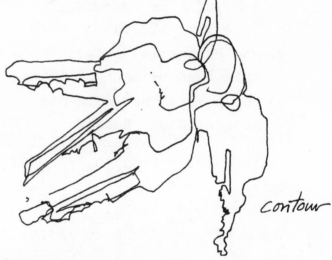

contour

Method: Place the point of the pencil or pen on your paper, put the object to the side so you cannot see the drawing. As you follow the contour of the object with your eye, simultaneously record what you see.

#3 Observation/Words

Another way to stimulate and heighten your awareness is to write at least ten descriptive words about an object. Write words that describe the texture or possibly a textile technique that is suggested.

INSPIRATION

Inspiration comes from innumerable sources. Seeing an object with renewed interest and recording it can develop a resource bank to 'draw on' for present and future ideas. (See contour drawing exercise.) The stimulus can come from an inner source (feelings, remembrances) or an outer source (nature, man-made). Everyone responds to various inspirations, so be open to your own direction. As you develop these preliminary skills you will be ready to move on to the phase of putting the concepts together.

= Exercises =

#1 Collecting Ideas

Take your sketch pad with you on a brief 'seeing' trip, and bring back ideas for several new garments.

Suggestions: Museum
                Art Gallery
                The Park
                Stationery
                Housewares
                (notice the
                dinnerware)
                Hardware

This would be a great time to try the contour drawing.

#2 Design Manipulation

Do the following exercise using one of the motifs or designs you've collected. The design, on the right, is the basis for all the ideas on this page.

A. Reduce it / Enlarge it

B. Repeat it

Pocket?

C. Seperate & rearrange it

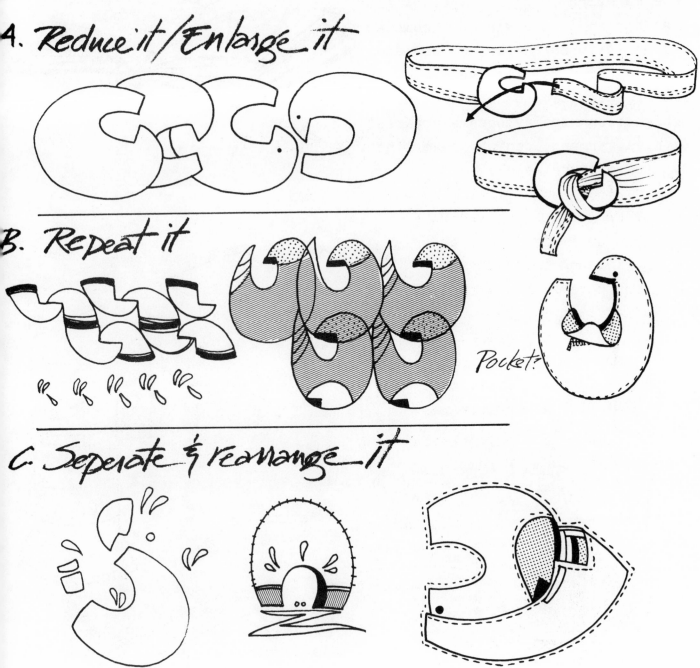

Using one of the shapes below,
trace outline on an extra sheet
of paper. Cut out, leaving the background intact. This 'window' can be
used effectively to pinpoint or locate
a design when placed over any picture
in a magazine or book. The designs
that appear in the window become exciting textures/shapes/ colors and
may suggest a textile technique. On
closer inspection other structural
design elements may become apparent
(i.e. a garment opening, seam lines,
type of closure, etc.)

#3 Cut-outs

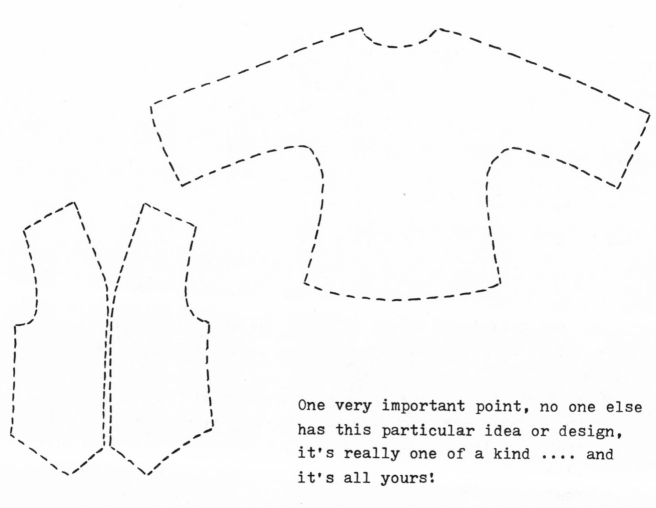

One very important point, no one else
has this particular idea or design,
it's really one of a kind .... and
it's all yours!

Stencil type cutout

These cut-outs are a wonderful 'tool' to use and you will find as you use it more, your ideas will come faster than you can act on them.

Suggestion: In your sketch book, trace around the cut-out shape several times. When you find an idea that appeals to you, draw the design on the traced shapes. This is a good reference when you need a fresh idea....your sketch pad will have a wealth of information in it.

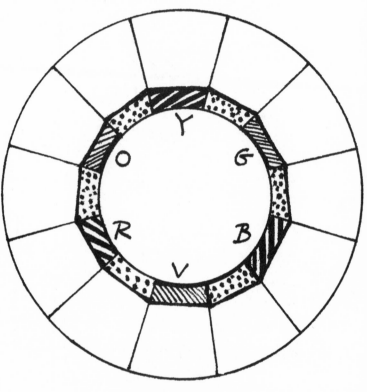

Color

One of the many decisions to be made regarding a garment is the color. Many people have one or two favorite colors that are comfortable and 'safe'. If this describes you, try starting with one of those colors, and adding a new one...such as, its complement or a triad scheme (see opposite page).

The color wheel is one easy way to acquaint yourself with various combinations of color. For easy reference color the wheel with colored pencils. Red, yellow, blue are the primary colors. The secondary colors are made by mixing equal parts of two of these to make the colors in between. Then the tertiary colors are made by mixing adjoining colors.

 RED
YELLOW
BLUE

 GREEN
VIOLET
ORANGE

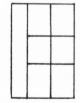 YELLOW GREEN
BLUE GREEN
BLUE VIOLET
RED VIOLET
RED ORANGE
YELLOW ORANGE

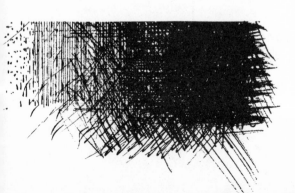

Value:

Lightness or darkness of a color is called value. Black or white is added to the color to change the value.

12

= Exercises =

#1 With fabric swatches: plan a garment or ensemble using each of these color schemes.

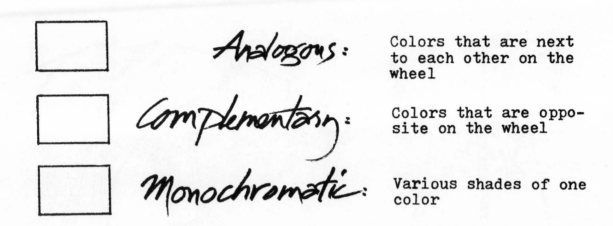

Analogous: Colors that are next to each other on the wheel

Complementary: Colors that are opposite on the wheel

Monochromatic: Various shades of one color

#2 Triad is one other color scheme you might like to try, it combines three colors equal distance apart on the wheel. When doing this exercise try for a good balance of value (light and dark) and intensity (bright and dull).

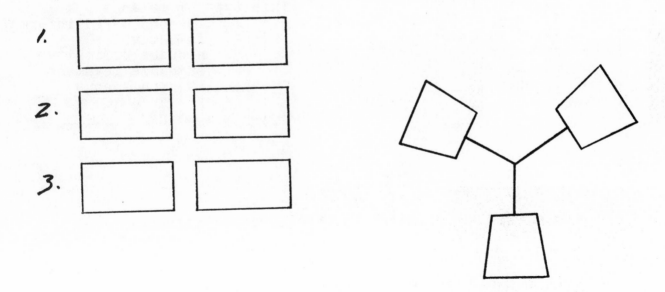

1.

2.

3.

Balance is the relationship of proportion between two or more
elements. The following examples are illustrations of this.

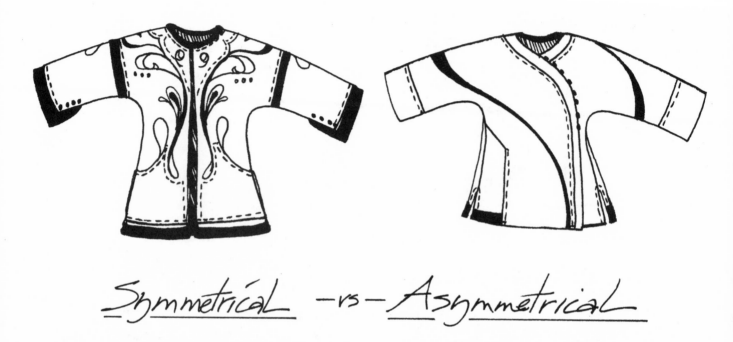

Symmetrical —vs— Asymmetrical

In symmetrical balance, each
half is a mirror image.
This type of balance

1. is more 'formal'
2. is passive
3. tends to stabilize
   a design
4. can be dull
5. is easy

In asymmetrical balance, the
weight (or attractions) on
each side are equal...but <u>not</u>
identical.
This type of balance

1. is considered informal
2. is active
3. arouses curiosity
4. suggests movement
5. is spontaneous

* Note: The human body illustrates both types of balance:

anterior and posterior view = symmetrical
the lateral view = asymmetrical

What an interesting form to design around!

Using the jacket and vest shape below, plan and sketch a
balanced design. The blank space can be used to draw your
own outline. The lines and design elements will emphasize
the **various** areas of your body....keep this in mind as your
plan takes shape.

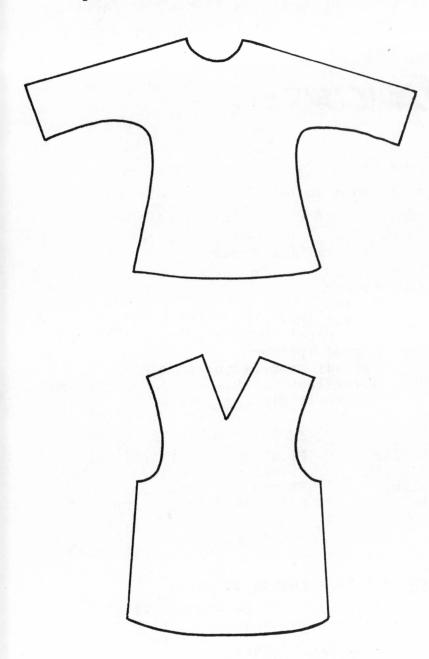

Clothing Analysis

The best time to organize your closet and analyze your wardrobe is at the beginning of the spring/summer and the fall/winter season. Try on everything in the closet to see what still fits, what may need mending, what needs replacing, etc. The following two exercises will help you assess your wardrobe. This information will be useful in making decisions. Try to be objective. Decide what looks good...and feels good... on you. Refer to these sheets when you buy ready-to-wear or fabric for garments. This plan may help to curb impulse buying and to channel your efforts in creating a very functional wardrobe.

= Exercises =

#1 Personal Analysis

Circle the styles that you consistently wear or ones that you relate to. This exercise is designed to help you evaluate your individual design details. Use this sheet for future reference.

Basic Dress

Sheath or shift
Blouson (belted)
Full skirt
Princess
Empire
A-line
Shirtwaist
Hem length _____

Basic Sleeve Shapes

Fitted/ set in
Kimono
Raglan
Dolman (bat-wing)
Drop shoulder/square
Capped (puffed)
Cuffed, gathered or straight
Sleeveless
Sleeve length _____

Necklines/ collars

Jewel (high neck)   Shawl Collar
V-neck   Notched Collar
Square   Flat Collar
Round (scoop)   Mandarin
Boat   Jabot
Keyhole   Ascot
Cardigan   Cowl

Pants

Pleated   Straight Leg
Fitted   Cuffed
Flared   With Pockets
Front or Back Closure

Accessories

Belts, scarves, hats, ties

Details   Closures   Skirts

Tucks   Buttons   Wrap-around   Straight
Pleats   Zippers   Gathered   Pleated
Gathers   Ties   Bias   A-line
Pockets   Other ____   Length _____

16

Wardrobe Analysis

For each season, make two copies of the wardrobe chart below. On one sheet fill in the appropriate boxes with the colors of the garments and accessories you now own. On the second sheet make notes on what you would like to add to your wardrobe to make it more complete.

OUTERWEAR	CASUAL	DRESSY	ACCESSORIES				
			Shoes	Bags	Belts		
Coats							
Jackets							
Vests							
INNERWEAR							
Dresses							
Pants							
Skirts							
Blouses							
Tops							

PART II

Translating

DEFINITIONS....

Translate: To change from one form or condition to another

Interpret: To regard from one's own viewpoint

Transform: To change the shape, character or appearance of

Balance: Composition or placement of elements of design in such a way as to produce a pleasing integrated whole.

Now you are ready to move into translating your designs. You may
wish to consider the surface and structural aspects. In relation
to surface design...are you reminded of any special techniques,
i.e. quilting, tucks, patchwork, that could be used on your garment? The structural design relates to the construction of the
garment. Does it work with a pattern you have and can adapt? We
encourage you to try 'straying' from commercial patterns and to
change the suggested decorative effects. Try using the ideas that
you work out for children's clothes, as well as adult garments.

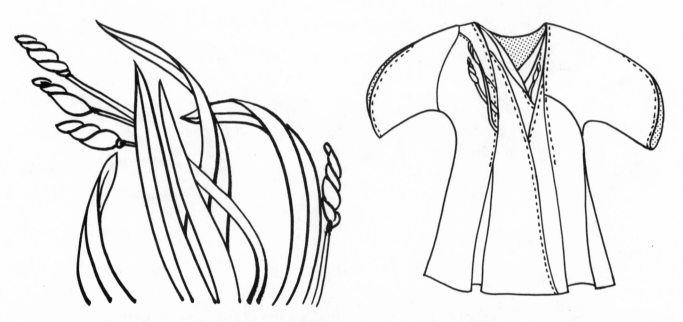

There are many aspects involved in designing a garment. There are
various approaches. Some tend to be inspired by the pattern...some
by the fabric....some by the technique to be used. A starting point
could even be the closure -- one interesting antique button, perhaps.

This is one of the most creative moments....getting your decisions
and your materials together. Ultimately these separate elements will
be all combined into one unified piece. The trim, accents, or focal
point of the piece need to relate to and be an integral part of the
whole garment...to look intentional as opposed to an afterthought.
The secret is to trust your judgement and begin. The more you do...
each little success...builds confidence and soon you will be translating with ease.

The following is a list of questions to ask yourself. Use
them to motivate, to get started or to refer back to when
you come to an impasse.

What is the major impression you wish to convey?

Is the style you've designed appropriate for the occasion?
                                    ....your body type?
                                    ....the season?
                                    ....the fabric?

Is the emphasis on the right part?

What areas of your figure would you like to accentuate?

Which areas would you like to deemphasize?

Which areas would you like to detract from?

Is the design being all that it needs to be?
                        .... can it be more?
                        .... can it be less?

How does the design relate to the other parts of the garment?

Is the design balanced?

Is the closure integrated into the overall design?

Are you trying to combine too many elements?
            (elements = color, texture, pattern)

Perhaps too few?

Are the materials appropriate for the effect?

Which material is dominant?

Which material is the accent?

Do these questions suggest a starting point?

Suggestion: <u>Start with the element you are sure of</u>.

Fresh and exciting ideas for garment designs are easily accessible. There are many historical costume books available thru your library or bookstore. Magazines of all descriptions offer a variety of inspiration. For a visual treat consider buying a foreign fashion magazine. To broaden your horizons we suggest visiting a museum, art gallery or maybe a foreign trade show. Exposing yourself to new and varied sources for ideas can prove stimulating and thought-provoking. Everytime we learn something new, we become something different.

Design Studies

The illustrations on the following pages are of costumes of a particular country or a period of time with suggestions for current ideas. These are just a sampling of garments to show some of the possibilities. The comments on these pages are presented as a point of departure, one more way to get your creativity 'in gear' and a good exercise to include in your designing procedure.

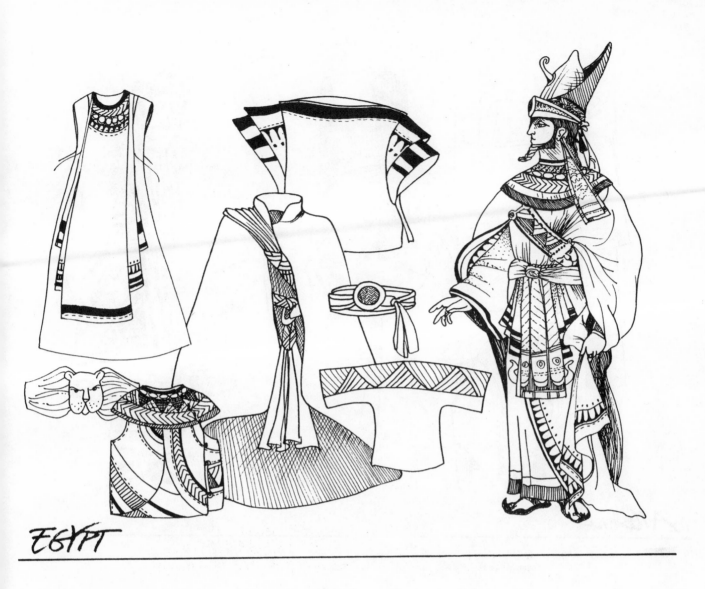

EGYPT

Design Analysis: Cape shape with patterned lining
                    Cloth gathered to or behind a firm band
                    Beaded yoke

Fabrics: Border Print
                    Quilted
                    Soft, drapes easily
                    Pleated

Techniques: Applique
                    Patchwork
                    Stenciled Borders
                    Pleated sculptural shapes (belts?)
                    Diagonal draped cloth (bias)
                    Layering with separate pieces

Albania

Design Analysis: Vest, applied bands, piecing
                    Deep armholes on vest
                    Asymetrical closing on A-line jacket
                    Mandarin collar
                    Full pleated sleeves on top
                    Inset piping on pants

Fabrics: Denim or textured cotton
                    Wool, felt
                    Soft leather or leather-like fabrics
                    Embroidered bands

Techniques: Patchwork
                    Piping
                    Pleats
                    Stencilling
                    Topstitching

YUGOSLAVIA

Design Analysis:	Full sleeves Inverted pleats on sides of dress/skirt 3/4 length straight vest, design on border Layering
Fabrics:	Cotton for dress Border print Silk for a dressy emsemble Light weight upholstery for vest

Techniques:	Vest: Seminole patchwork
	        Quilting
	        Applique
	        Topstitching
	Blouse:Embroidery
	        Painted Fabric
	Rope ties, draw strings

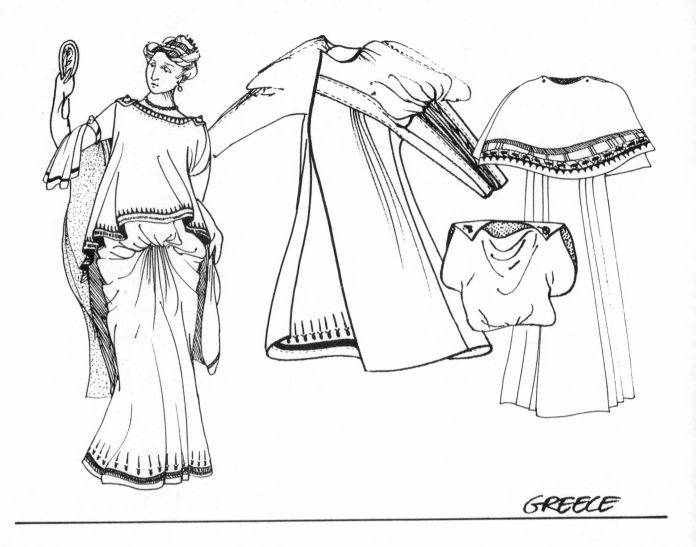

GREECE

Design Analysis: Soft
                    Bias cut
                    Fastens on the shoulder
                    Layered garments
                    Large rectangle of soft fabric
Fabric: drawn together to accentuate
                        a line

Fabric: Silk or polyester crepe de chine
                    Gauze
                    Pleated

Techniques: Stenciled design
                    Knot buttons/loops
                    Embroidery
                    Seminole Patchwork

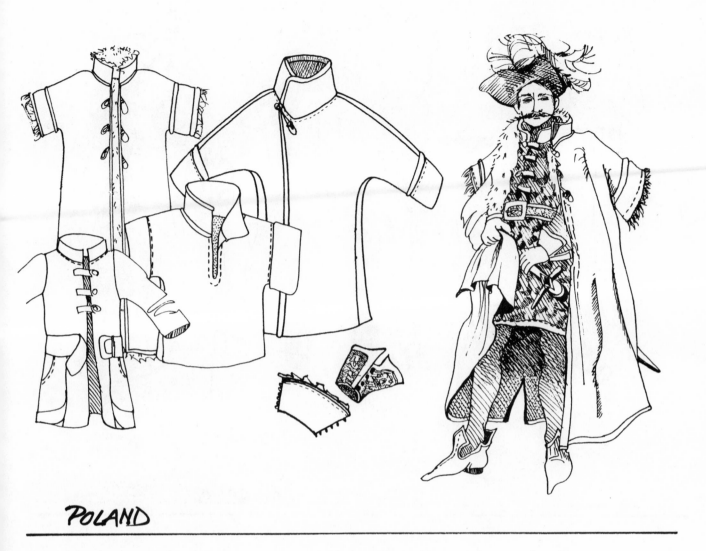

POLAND

Design Analysis: Fleece lined coat
                   Tapestry tunic
                   Toggle fasteners
                   Stand-up collar
                   Cuff detail
                   Fitted pants (bias?)

Fabric: Embroidered or woven 'tapestry' fabric
                   Melton wool for coat
                   Sheepskin for lining or just for cuffs
                       and collar
                   Bias for trim

Techniques: Piping
                   Stitched design, double needle
                   Covered cording
                   Sections of woven strips
                   Frogs
                   Leather buttons

HOLLAND

Design Analysis:	Wrapped belt
	Pants with bib
	Layering
	Prints and solids
	Important pockets
Fabric:	Cotton knits
	Denim
	Lace collar
Techniques:	Roped sash
	Piping
	Corded ties
	Piecing
	Decorative tacks
	In-seam pockets

ANCIENT ROME

Design Analysis: Pliable but firm looking vest
Pleated skirt
Horizontal and vertical lines
    to consider
Asymetrical closing

Fabrics: Quilted
Prints and plain cottons combined
Leather
Denim

Techniques: Quilting
Shaped piecing with bias edge
Stitching

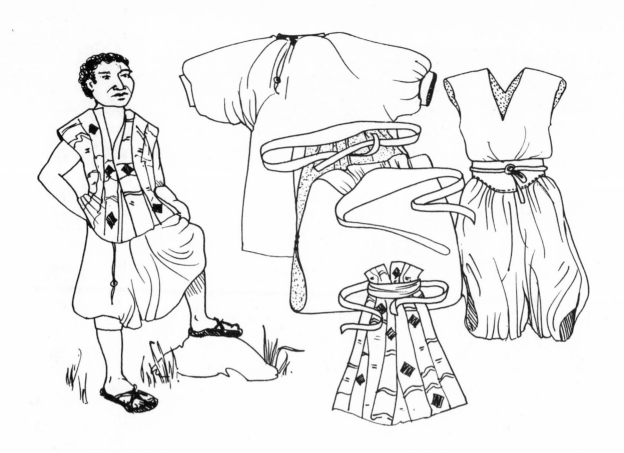

AFRICA

Design Analysis: Very full gathered pants
                    Wide cuffs, could be embroidered
                    Triangular insets on shirt
                    Piecing

Fabrics: Fine cotton for voluminous pants
                    Elegant for evening, i.e. silk

Techniques: Embroidery
                    Smocking
                    Gussets
                    Piping

GERMANY

Design Analysis: Hooded vest
                        Accentuated armholes
                        Shaped Hem

Fabrics: Knitted undergarment
                        Corduroy vest
                        Wool vest
                        Printed facings and/or lining

Techniques: Shaped facings to the outside
                        Piping
                        Wrinkled and stitched

31

CANADA

Design Analysis:	Cape/coat outer garment Boat neckline Yoked pants
Fabrics:	Striped cotton Leather Printed borders
Techniques:	Inset piecing Tassels Shaped Hems Ribbon embroidery

CHINA

Design Analysis: 'Caped' sleeve overgarment
Raglan sleeve
Asymetrical Closure
Frogs
Pieced design border
3/4 length tunic/ long skirt

Fabrics: Border print
Pleated
Soft, i.e silk, satin

Techniques: Piecing
Piping
Shaped facings
Pleats/tucks
Yarn beads
Frogs

GERMANY

Design Analysis: Sculptural collar
                     Short cape...shaped layers
                     Cuffed pants

Fabrics: Wool or corduroy for cape
                     Silky lining
                     Striped challis for pants

Techniques: Shaped layering
                     Piping
                     Strip weaving
                     Trapunto

34

ALASKA

Design Analysis:	Pieced dress/coat Patchwork using all one color fabric Seams are important Cuffs on full sleeves
Fabrics:	Skins 'Suede' or 'leather' fabrics Felt Wool Raw silk
Techniques:	Topstitching Faggoting Embroidery Piping

TURKEY

Design Analysis:	Burnoose, loose cape-like garment Layered full length garments Full skirt
Fabrics:	Cottons Lace Antique fabrics Lightweight wool
Techniques:	Seminole patchwork Topstitching Striped bias piping Fabric inset in 'window'

JAPAN

Design Analysis: Neckline..Design focus
                    Pleated scarf
                    Jacket, full sleeves
                    Sashes, printed lining

Fabrics: Soft ...Fine cottons, silk
                    Pleated
                    Vest: Firm
                              Basketry materials
                              Handmade felt

Techniques: Diagonal stitching on sleeves
                            (double needle)
                    Pleating
                    Inset fabric in 'window'
                    Piecing

RUMANIA

Design Analysis: Decorated overcoat
                     Cuffed pants
                     Full sleeved shirt
                     Wide belt

Fabrics: 'Leather' or 'suede' like fabrics
                          for appliques
                     Felt
                     Ribbon trim

Techniques: Applique
                     Piecing
                     Topstitching
                     'Windows'
                     Decorative tacks

AMERICA 1800's

Design Analysis: Lace layers
                    Bias, fitted skirt
                    Kimino sleeve
                    Cinched waist, with belt

Fabrics: Lace
                    Antique fabrics
                    Elegant fabrics i.e. satin, silk

Techniques: Shaped piecing
                    Decorative tacks
                    Beading
                    Loose layers
                    Tucks/pleats

JAPAN

Design Analysis:	Wrapped front top
	Layered jacket
	Wrapped belt
	Quilted shoulder pieces
	Pleated pants
Fabrics:	Print and solid fabrics
	Quilted
	'Silky' fabric for twisted belt
Techniques:	Roped ties
	Piping
	Quilting
	Pleats/tucks inset in sleeve bands

SIBERIA

Design Analysis: Hooded Coat
                    A-line
                    Inset sleeve yoke pieces
                    Border detailing

Fabrics: Skins
                    Sheepskin
                    Felt
                    Melton Wool
                    Printed fabrics

Techniques: Piping
                    'Windows'
                    Shaped piecing
                    Tucks
                    Topstitching

41

MEXICO

Design Analysis:	Loose fitting tops Embroidered blouse Slit neckline with tassels Full skirts
Fabrics:	Cotton Handwoven cotton would be perfect Twill weaves would be interesting
Techniques:	Wrapping Tassels Embroidery Tucks/pleats for skirt

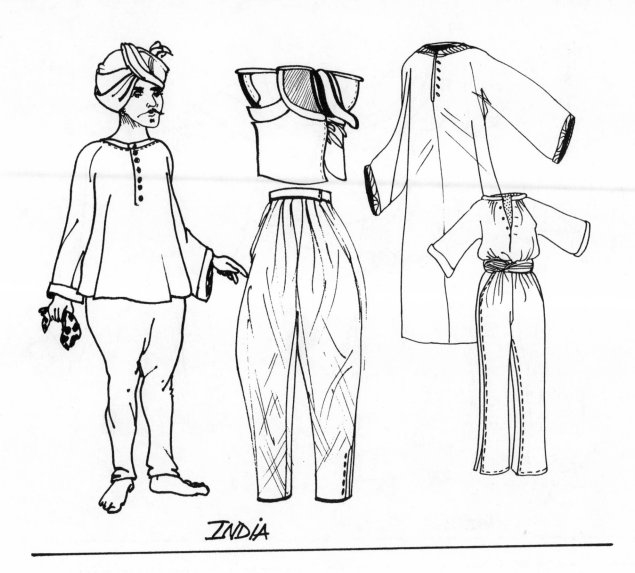

INDIA

Design Analysis:	Flared, A-line top Boat neck Bias, full pants Wrapped belt
Fabrics:	Natural fibers, i.e. raw silk, textured cotton Knits Print for lining, piping, sleeve bands
Techniques:	Piping Topstitching Yarn beads Buttons made from beads

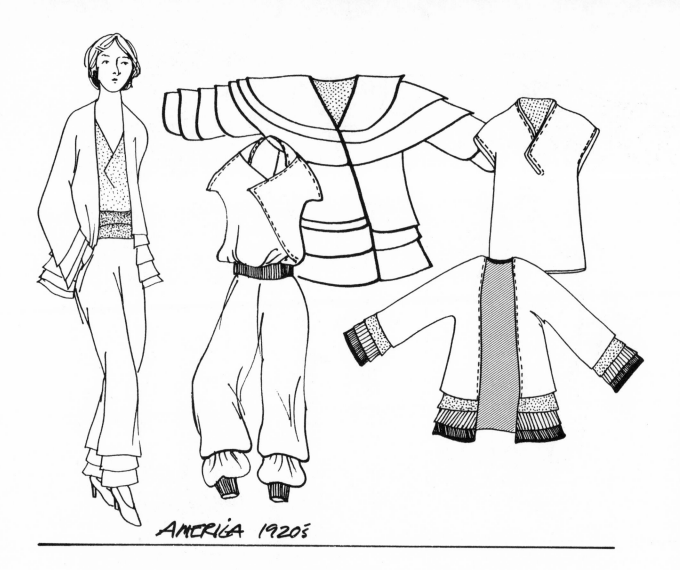

AMERICA 1920s

Design Analysis:	Layered jacket Lap front camisole Cuffed pants with horizontal pleats
Fabrics:	Soft fabrics, i.e. cotton or silk Knits Crepe de Chine
Techniques:	Tucks Beading Piping Decorative Stitching

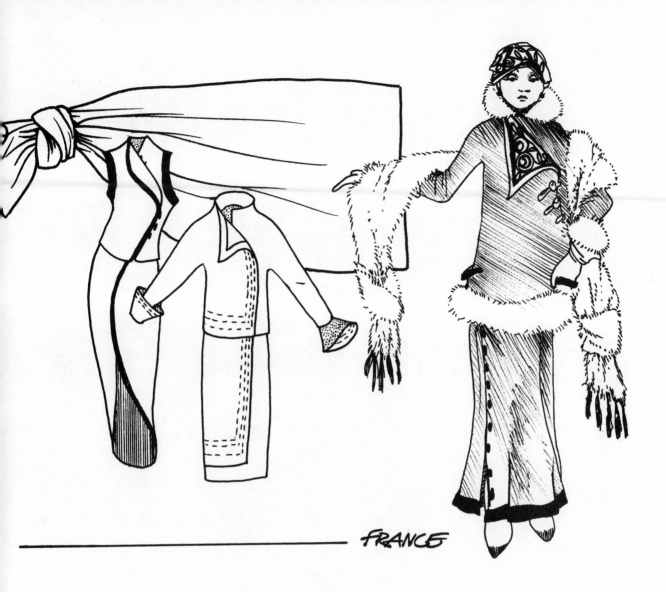

FRANCE

Design Analysis: Fur trimmed suit
Print lining
Piped with contrasting print
Dolman sleeves
Straight skirt

Fabrics: Gabardine
Wool
Textured silk
Silk print for trim

Techniques: Frogs
Piping
Buttonhole Pockets
Topstitching

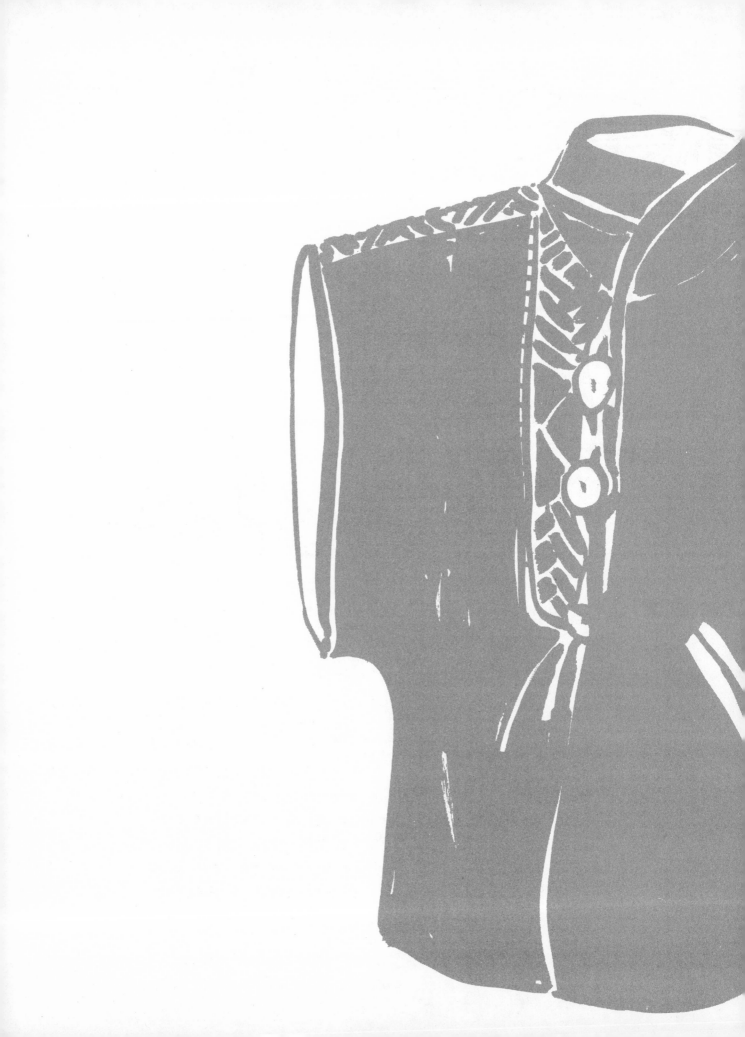

PART III

Sewing Techniques

DEFINITIONS....

Sew: To attach, join, make re-
            pair, enclose, or secure
            with stitches

Texture: The characteristic visual
            and tactile quality of the
            surface of a work of art re-
            sulting from the way in which
            the materials are used.

Fastener: Any of various devices for
            holding together two objects
            or parts sometimes required
            to be separate, as the two
            edges or flaps of a piece of
            clothing

Bias Binding

Bias bindings are more than just a functional way to finish an edge; they are probably one of the most verstile ways to use fabric. These bindings can accentuate and emphasize the lines of your garment.

Try combining various textures for interest, i.e. velveteen with satin binding, or plain wool with striped silk binding. Also consider using a fabric with a distinct right/wrong...one side for the garment, the reverse for the binding. For added interest, piping can be inserted between the binding and the garment. Usually bias binding is flat, however, you could stuff this binding for a rounded effect. In addition to finishing an edge or seam, bias is used for applique, woven strips, and a variety of closures.

1.

To cut 'true' bias....
If you need a small strip or only have a small piece of fabric...use this method.

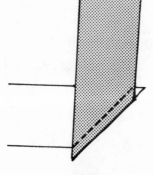

2.

1. Cut the fabric on the straight grain.

2. Fold it so the selvage is parallel to this cut edge.

3. Measure and mark the desired width for as many strips as you need.

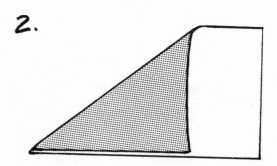

3.

4. Join the strips, as shown, right sides together.

5. Press seams open.

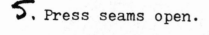

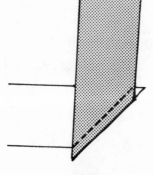

4.

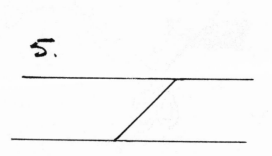

5.

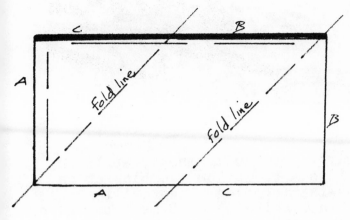

In a continuous tube :

The advantage of making a continuous tube is that after sewing and pressing just one seam, a very long bias strip is ready for use. This method is easier if you start with ½ yard of fabric, or more.

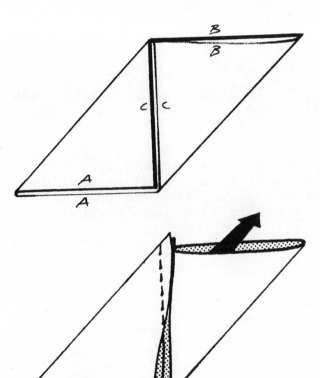

1. Fold on the lines as the diagram shows, matching the letters.

2. Pin and stitch the "c's" together.

3. Press seam open. This is now a tube.

4. Start cutting at one end of the tube. Each time before you flip the tube over, make a small cut with your scissors to mark the width of the strip. This helps to gauge where to cut...a destination, so to speak.

5. The first and last triangle will be trimmed off.

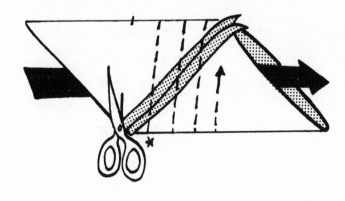

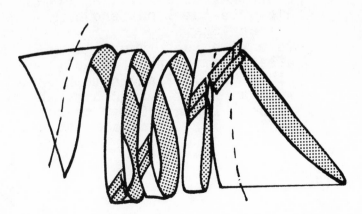

Tubes—

Tubes can be used in a variety of ways...for buttonloops, applique, ties, straps, or weaving. The fabric can be cut on the bias or on straight grain...lengthwise or crosswise (consider when cutting: crosswise may have more 'stretch' than lengthwise). Bias tubes have the most 'stretch' so these are best to use on curves. Printed fabrics, especially stripes, could have unusual effects when they are cut on the bias.

Method:

Cut the stips three times wider than the finished tube. If you want long pieces, stitch several cut strips together. Then fold in half and stitch, as shown. Note: if the fabric is thick or has a nap, long pieces may be difficult to turn.

No need to trim the seams. Make an indention at the end that has been stitched closed. Put the turning tool (see below) in that depression. Slide the fabric tube onto the tool. Cut off the very end, the one that was stitched. Press strips with the lengthwise seam in the middle of the back of the strip.

It is very easy to turn the tubes if you have some kind of a long smooth tool for that purpose. Alternatives to making a tool could be a chopstick or a knitting needle (use the blunt end).

To make a tool, you will need a 15"-20" piece of #9 galvanized wire. Flatten both ends with a hammer. Smooth rough places with a grinder or coarse sand paper. It's ready to use.

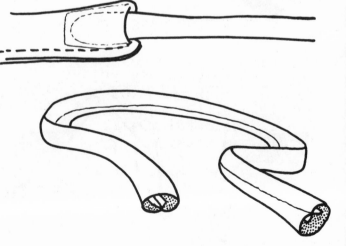

Cording, covered in a constrasting, printed or matching fabric can be used for knot buttons, loops, frogs or trimming.

Method:

Method:

1. Cut bias strips generously to 'go around' the cording you've chosen. Remember it is easier to trim it later.

2. Measure the length of bias from one end of the cording. No..... don't cut it! Now pin your bias, wrong side out, to the second length of cording.

3. Using a zipper foot, stitch across the cording and bias, then stitch along the cording all the way down the side. Be careful not to catch the cording in the stitching.

4. Trim close to the stitching.

5. Draw the cording out of the bias.

6. Voila'...it's covering the first length of cording. Now when you cut it off, the remainder of the cording will be all one piece.

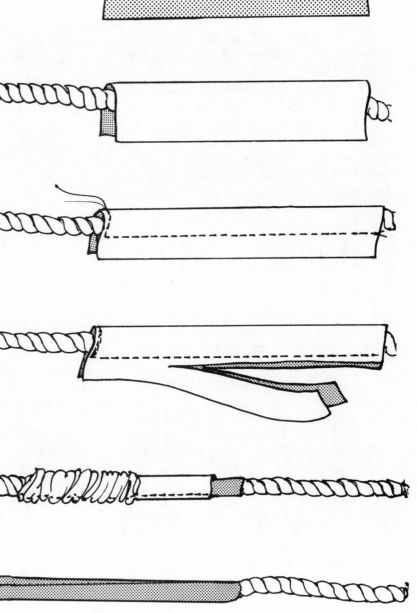

Corded piping lends a special tailored accent to your sewing. For added interest you may wish to try a contrasting color or an unusual print. Commercial patterns are using piping more and more as a decorative element. Piping can be purchased by the yard or package.... you can also make it in the fabric of your choice.

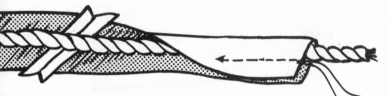

1. Cut the strips of bias at least four times the width of the cord to be covered. It is much easier to handle a wider strip, even if you waste some.

2. Fold it over the cording, right side out. Leave one side narrower than the other to eliminate extra bulk in the seams.

3. Using a zipper foot, stitch close to the cord, using a basting stitch.

To add interest to your piping, strips of fabric or ribbon can be applied, see diagram 3. To apply...if using fabric strips, the edges should be pressed under but not sewn. Fold ribbon or fabric strips over the bias piping. Pin in place and stitch as you are making the piping.

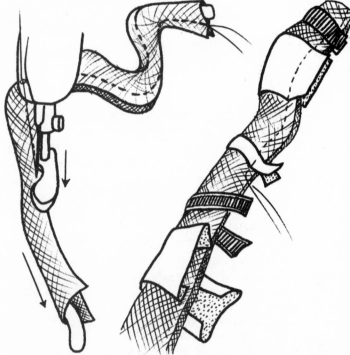

To apply piping to the garment: pin the cording to the edge of the fabric at the seam allowance and stitch using the zipper foot. Stitch from the bias side, so you can use the other stitching line as a guide. Place the companion pieces of the garment together. Pin in place, right sides together. Stitch thru all thicknesses, using the previous stitching as a guide.

> Note: Using the stitching lines as a guide assures an even professional look.
> Also clip the curves and corners, where it is needed, as you would any other seam.

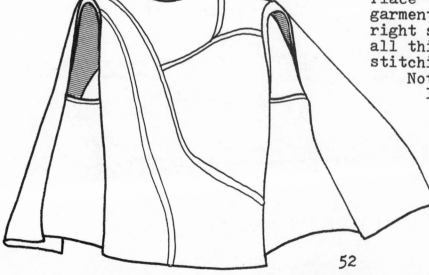

Wrapped Cording

It is easy to make your own wrapped cording. This is an excellent technique to add to your skills. It can be used for handles on a purse, frogs, soft jewelry (a beautiful necklace can be made with very few beads...also it is lightweight and comfortable to wear).

Perle cotton, embroidery thread, or silk floss work well to wrap 'with'. Covered cording or other cord that does not have a very definite twist to it, work well to wrap 'on'.

Method:

1. Pin the end of the cording to a piece of cardboard or tie it to a chair to give a little tension.

2. Place the end of the thread you're wrapping with parallel with the cording. Wrap around tightly and evenly until the desired length is reached. Place a needle, with a large eye, parallel to the cording with the eye toward the direction you are wrapping. Wrap over needle

3. and cording for about ½". Thread the needle with the end of the thread and pull thru to fasten. Cut the thread.

4. To add a new thread, hold the ending thread with the cord, place the new thread as in the first step.

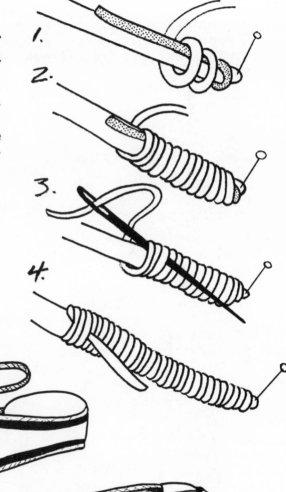

Roped Cords

This is a great way to make ties that match or contrast with your garment. To match your garment exactly, use the ravellings from your fabric. Some fabrics will be easier to ravel than others, of course. Other materials to consider for the roped cords could be perle cotton, yarn, embroidery thread, buttonhole twist or a variety of threads together.

Hand Method:

If you have no mechanical means to twist the threads, make an oval with the threads. Place a pencil or stick at each end (see detail); one person holds each stick and turns it in opposite directions to twist the threads. (You can also fasten one end to a doorknob.)

Mechanical Method:

Tie a knot at one end of the group of threads. Fasten with a string to the bobbin winder on your machine, the beater on your mixer or tape it to a drill bit.

Technique:

Measure threads...twice the length and half the width you want to end up with. Twist, keeping tension on the end, use one of the methods suggested. Twist test...to see if you have enough twist 'fold' the threads, let it twist back on itself...if it seems firm, it's probably all right...if not, twist a little more. Fold in half or place a weight in the middle, allow to spin into a rope. Tie off loose ends. Fasten to your garment, either in a seam or sew it on top, where desired. The knotted or 'folded' end could be the end of the tie.

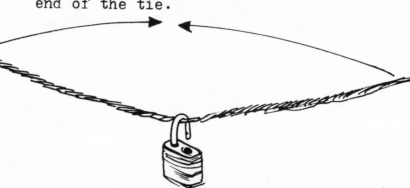

54

Closures

.....or, look at the button rack last.
In this chapter we want to encourage your imagination
to soar! To turn an object into part of a fastener is
a challenge. It could be helpful to keep this thought
in mind: LOOK AT SOMETHING FOR WHAT IT IS...NOT WHAT
IT'S CALLED. The reason for this is, when an object
gets 'named'...the potential for use is limited.

Mark the placement for the loops. Wrap the cording around the button to determine the length of the cording for each loop. Cut each loop accordingly. Position loops on the right side of the fabric and pin in place. Machine or hand baste. With the right sides together, position facing on the garment and stitch. Trim, turn and press.

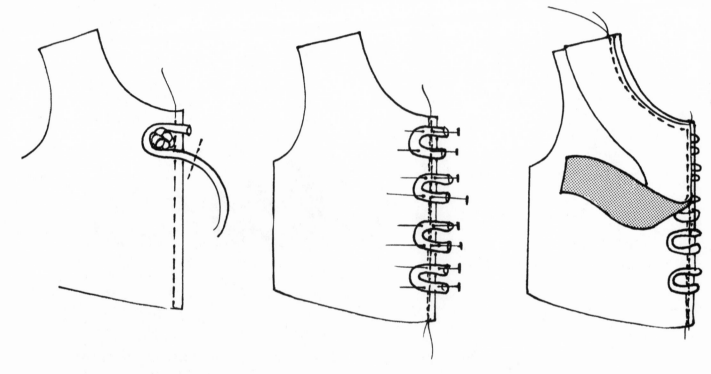

Additional stitching, very close to the seams, after trimming, with the seam allowance toward the facing...will keep the edge flat, turn easily and it will 'roll' nicely.

To make an easy buttonloop that matches your fabric, unravel a dozen or so threads from your left-over material. Twist these threads together, hold them taut and zig-zag over the twisted threads. Use these as buttonloops.

You can also use ribbon or pre-made cording of all descriptions for your loops.

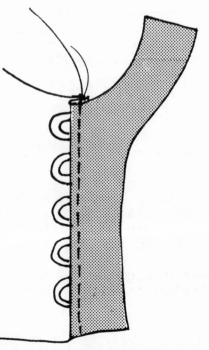

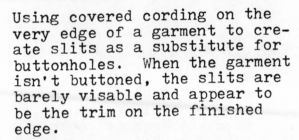

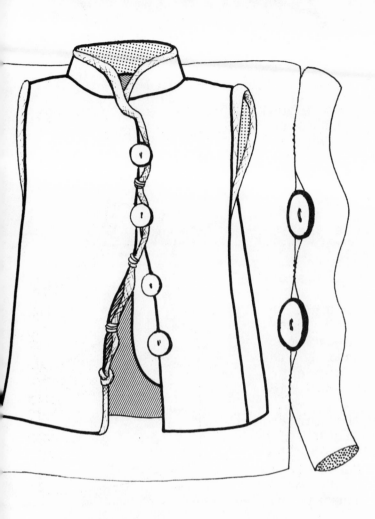

Using covered cording on the very edge of a garment to create slits as a substitute for buttonholes. When the garment isn't buttoned, the slits are barely visable and appear to be the trim on the finished edge.

Method: Cover 1/8" cording with bias fabric to match your garment, or use commercial cording available in fabric stores in a matching or contrasting color.

On the finished edge of the garment, mark the placement of the 'buttonholes' with pins. Hand-sew the cording to the very edge of the garment opening between the markings, leaving the slits slightly larger than the buttons.

A suggestion for added texture is to make a few overhand knots in the cording as you apply it along the garment edge remembering to allow extra length in the cording for the knots. To relate these knots to the garment, French knots could be embroidered on the cording in a matching color.

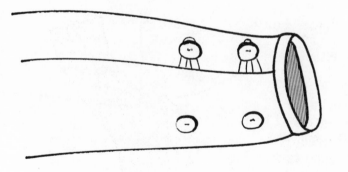

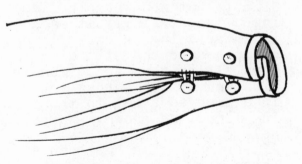

It is easy to make a cuff adjustable for a loose fitting or tight band at the wrist. Simply stitch two (or more) buttonloops in the seam, as shown. Sew two buttons to align with those loops. Then sew two more buttons in the appropriate place to draw it in tight when buttoned.

Other design areas where you might wish to employ this concept, in addition to cuffs, could be pants cuffs, necklines or waistbands.

Bound Buttonholes:

This is one of the easiest ways to make bound buttonholes. This technique could also be used to make handsome pockets. It works best with crisp, tightly woven fabrics. It is adviseable to interface the garment for added stability.

1. Baste the interfacing to the garment. Baste or mark lines for the buttonhole placement.
2. Cut a strip of fabric 1½" x (twice the finished buttonhole length plus 2"). Note: at this stage you may wish to interface, pad, or cord this strip, which will become the 'lips' of the buttonhole.
3. Fold the strip in half lengthwise and stitch 1/8" to 3/8" from the folded edges. The width between the fold and the stitching line will be the finished width of the buttonhole 'lips'. Trim off the cut edge so there is the same distance on each side of the stitching line.
4. Baste strips to the outside of the garment, raw edges together along the buttonhole line. The strips should extend ½" past both ends. Using small stitches, 10-12 per inch, sew the marked buttonhole length using the prestitched lines on the strips as a guide.
5. On the wrong side of the garment, carefully slash buttonhole opening as shown. Clip <u>to</u> but not <u>thru</u> the last stitch leaving a long triangle at each end. If there is interfacing or underlining, trim these off close to the stitching line.
6. Turn strips thru the slash to the wrong side and stitch across the triangle ends in a line adjacent to the first two stitching lines, as shown. Whipstitch buttonhole closed, then press.
7. After the facing has been stitched on, baste thru all thicknesses in a circle around the buttonhole to keep in place. Put a pin at each end of the buttonhole, so you can see where to cut a slit on the facing side. Cut the slit, leaving a long triangle as you did before, turn the raw edges under, hemstitch to hold in place.

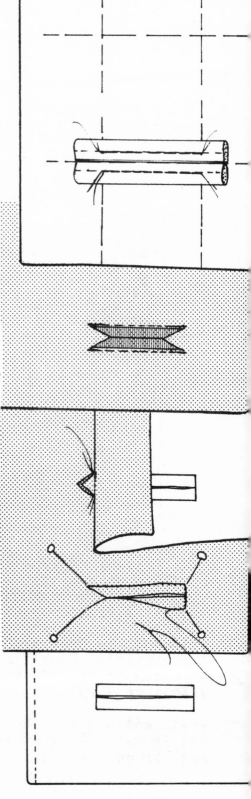

Hand Sewn Buttonholes:

Baste two vertical lines on the fabric the
width of the buttonholes.

1. Baste a line, as indicated, as a guide
and re-inforcement for the buttonhole
stitch.

2. Slash between the vertical lines.

3. Using buttonhole twist, or other heavy
duty thread, fill in the space with buttonhole stitches...very close together.

In-Seam Buttonholes:

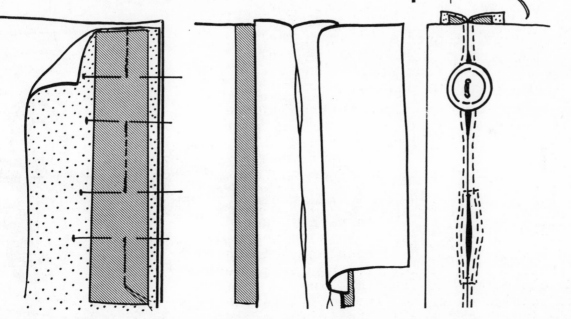

1. Use lightweight iron-on interfacing, if appropriate for your fabric,
or baste other interfacing in place. This strip would vary in size
(if your fabric is sheer you would want to interface the whole tab).
Otherwise, a narrow strip would probably be sufficient.
To mark buttonholes, place pins horizontally, indicating the desired
width of the opening. Stitch between the buttonholes.

2. Fold band back and tack in place. If lining is used stitch to seam
allowance only.

3. Press and top stitch, as shown, or any way you wish. The top stitching is necessary, at least around the hole, for re-inforcement. The
rest is decorative.

59

frogs

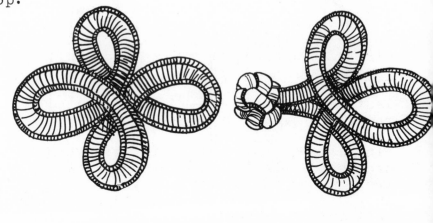

Frogs were originally called 'froggings'
or 'brandenburgs' and ornately fastened
military uniforms. Frogs are now widely
used for garments from casual to evening
wear.

Depending on the size of the cording,
you will need approximately 1½ yards for
a set (two pieces).

Make a knot button at one end, leaving a
two inch 'tail', as shown.

Step 1. Bring the long end over to form
a loop.
Step 2. Fasten with a thread to secure.
Repeat these two steps three more times
to form a flower shape. This will be
the back...turn it over and fasten the
frog to the garment. The other half of
the frog will have four petals, one of
which will be the buttonloop.

How to make a frog with
a toggle...a rod shaped
button.
Start the frog the same
as above. The last loop
will be left longer than
the rest of the loops.
This loop should be long
enough to cross and but-
ton to the toggle on the
opposite side. Make two
and fasten, as shown.

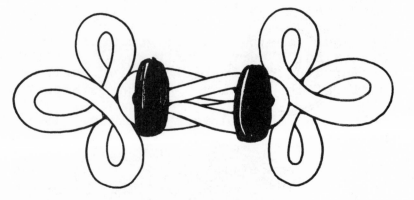

figure-8 Style:

When making this frog keep a figure '8' in mind. Make an '8' with
a small loop at the top and a little larger loop at the bottom. The
first end is passive throughout...its only function is to regulate
the size of the loop when it becomes the buttonhole. The size of the
loop at the bottom of the '8' depends on the size of the cording. You
will be able to judge the loop size after a few practice ones.

With the long end, start on the second figure '8', with the top of the
'8' wrapping snugly around the 'neck' (see diagram). As it comes
around the front...always in a figure '8' motion...fill the lower
circle in with another loop of cording. Come around the 'neck' again,
lower than the first one, then fill in the lower circle with another
loop. Then around the 'neck' (3rd and last time)...lower than the
last and put this end into the smallest circle at the bottom..at this
point the frog should stay together.

Pin the ends together on the back. Leave both ends uncut until you
decide how big the buttonloop is going to be. To finish, stitch the
two ends on the back and take a few stitches to keep the lower circles
in place. To make the button side of the frog, begin or end with the
knot button. To use a figure '8' frog as a tie...in place of the buttonhole and button...simply leave the first end long enough to tie.

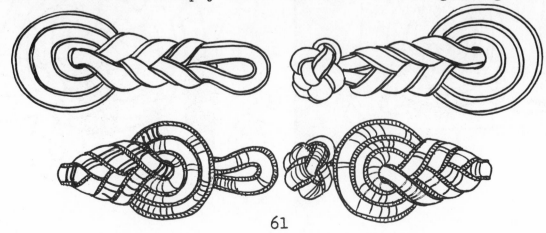

Ideas for various frogs or other knotted fasteners can come from many sources. Here are a few ideas to investigate as starting points:

a. Old metal jewelry has interesting designs...all cultures, all eras, i.e. the Celts and the Vikings

b. Some old books have intricate borders on each page

c. Metal work on armor and the helmets could be an inspirational source

d. Nature photography...i.e. vines, seaweed or grasses that intertwine

e. Nautical books...with knotted ropes

There are a variety of materials to choose from to make corded types of fasteners. A few ideas, besides cordings, are braids, and trims, rounded leather cords, velvet ribbon, thin ropes. The design you have chosen could be just a series of loops, stitched in place. The buttonloop can be made where needed. Small objects, i.e. Chinese coins or beads, could be added where desired.

When you design your own frogs, one method for experimenting might be to draw your design on paper. Place the cording on the paper...pin in position. Fasten together. Hand sew the frog in place.

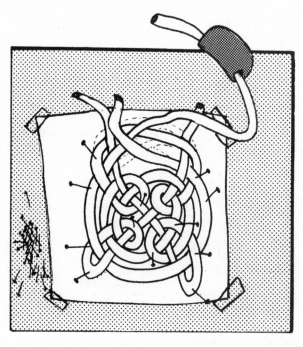 

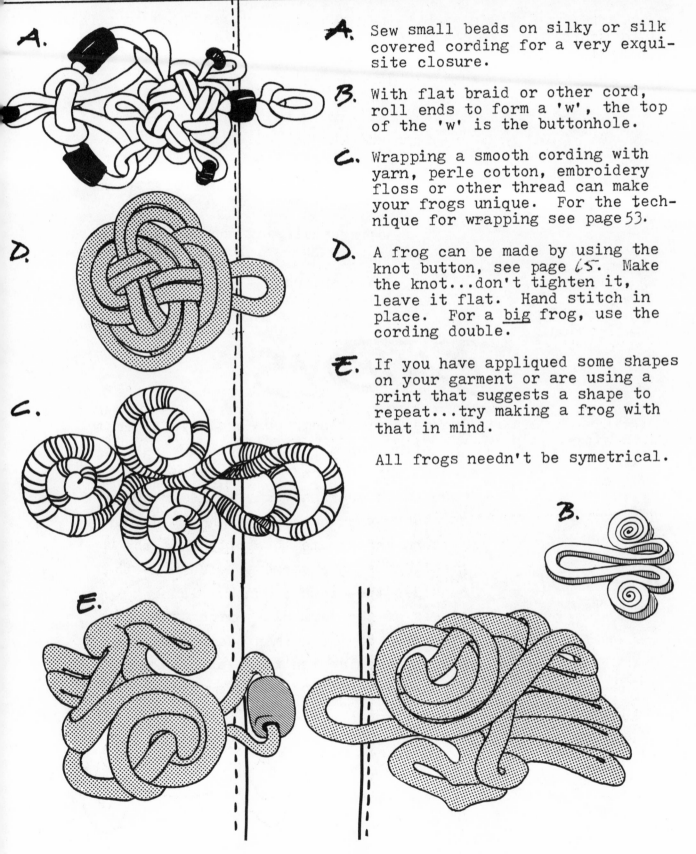

A. Sew small beads on silky or silk covered cording for a very exquisite closure.

B. With flat braid or other cord, roll ends to form a 'w', the top of the 'w' is the buttonhole.

C. Wrapping a smooth cording with yarn, perle cotton, embroidery floss or other thread can make your frogs unique. For the technique for wrapping see page 53.

D. A frog can be made by using the knot button, see page 65. Make the knot...don't tighten it, leave it flat. Hand stitch in place. For a <u>big</u> frog, use the cording double.

E. If you have appliqued some shapes on your garment or are using a print that suggests a shape to repeat...try making a frog with that in mind.

All frogs needn't be symetrical.

Button: A small disc or knob for attach-
         ing to an article of clothing;
         being small and round, as orna-
         ment; to insert in a button-
         hole or loop

The definition sets our creative thoughts
in motion for a possible closure select-
ion. Since buttons add the finishing
touches to your garment, it is important
to choose them carefully. Analyze your
pattern and relate the buttons to the
'feeling' of the garment. You need to
consider the closure in the planning
stages of the garment. During the construction of the garment sometimes we
feel the design isn't quite 'clicking'--
the perfect button could be the unify-
ing element.

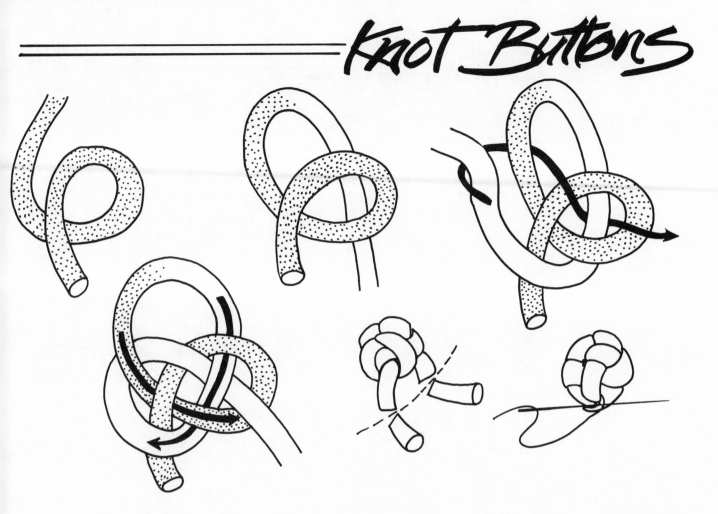

Use a length of cording, at least 1/4" wide...3/8" makes a large size button.
Make a 6 with the short tail on the top of the 6. Make a second loop and place it behind the first, so it looks like a pretzel. Now take the long end and lay it on top of the tail of the 6.

Now weave under, over, under, over across the pretzel. At this point the knot should stay together.

To tighten... hold the two ends with your little fingers, and pull on the two center loops in the direction of the arrows. Then ease the loops closed. Tightening them too quickly, make the balls irregular. This takes a little practice, but is well worth it. Cut the cording off about 3/4" from the end, sew ends together, as shown. Tuck these ends inside the ball and fasten together. Leaving the threaded needle on the end of each ball button, makes it easy to sew it to the garemnt.

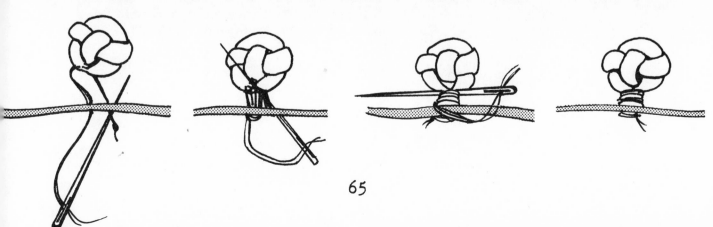

Leather Buttons

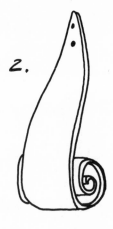

1. Cut a triangle, about 3" long, depending on the thickness of the leather or suede.

2. Punch 2 small holes, or use a hammer and a nail to make the holes...at the narrow end, to sew it to the garment.

3. Run a line of fabric or leather glue on the center of the triangle. Roll the triangle, tightly from the wide end and make a mark where the slits will be cut.

4. The punched point is inserted through the slit and the button is sewn in place.

fabric Buttons

1.

2.

3.

Here are some suggestions for use with commercial covered-button kits.

1. Stitch small tucks, randomly or in a pattern.

2. Cut circles of embroidered fabric i.e. old tablecloth or embroider some circles yourself.

3. Stitch soutache braid to fabric, cut circles and make buttons.

Yarn Beads or Buttons

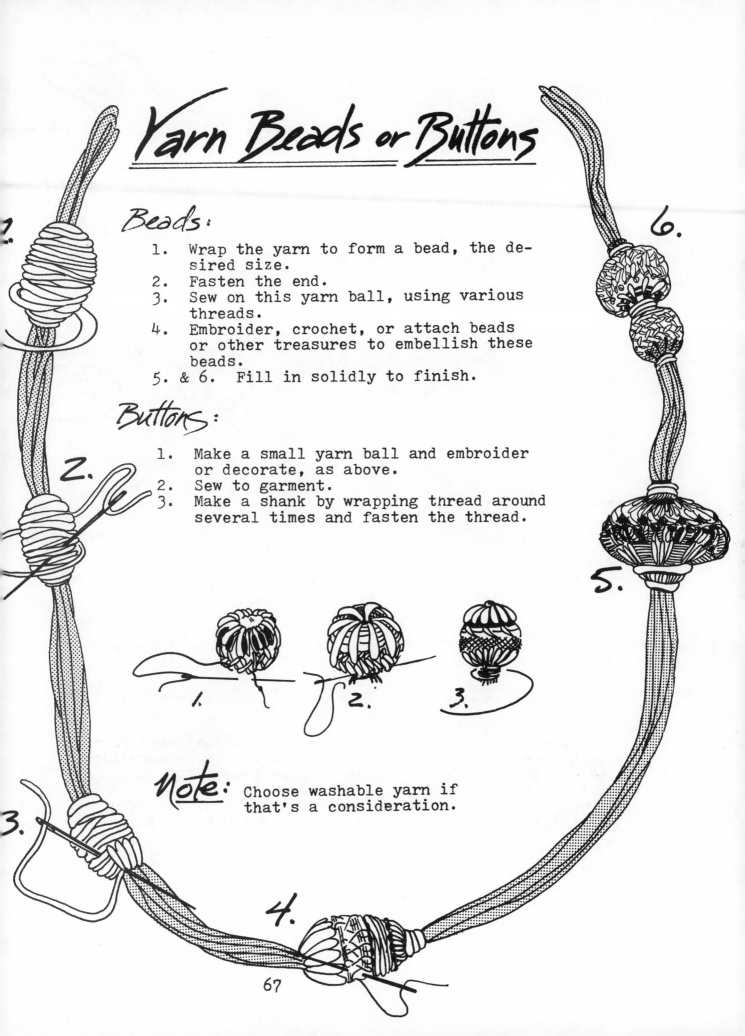

Beads:

1. Wrap the yarn to form a bead, the desired size.
2. Fasten the end.
3. Sew on this yarn ball, using various threads.
4. Embroider, crochet, or attach beads or other treasures to embellish these beads.
5. & 6. Fill in solidly to finish.

Buttons:

1. Make a small yarn ball and embroider or decorate, as above.
2. Sew to garment.
3. Make a shank by wrapping thread around several times and fasten the thread.

Note: Choose washable yarn if that's a consideration.

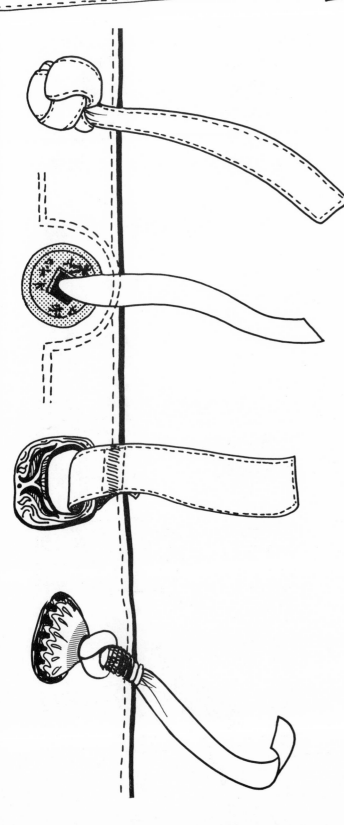

As in drawing a line --- you only need to be concerned with beginnings and endings of a tie --- those are the punctuation points ---the middle will take care of itself.

Some of these ideas can be the beginnings and endings, also add your own.

Consider the parts of a garment that need or could use a fastener...maybe that closure could be a tie?

- ...to close a pocket
- ...to cinch in the pant legs
- ...to use as 'cuffs' on sleeves
- ...to fasten a purse or make a handle for one
- ...to fasten a neckline
- ...to replace a collar
- ...to use as a belt, or partial belt across the back of a vest, for instance

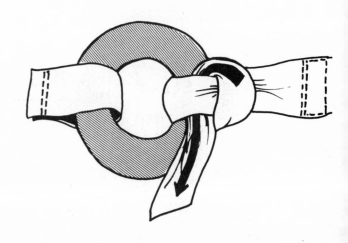

Looped Tie:

This fastener is made of cording. The length of the right loop depends on the diameter of the narrow object that will fasten the loops together. This narrow object could be a piece of bamboo, wood or bone....

Consideration: a smooth object will be easy to pull thru and will keep the cording from fraying or wearing.

The loop on the left side need only be large enough for the right loop to pass thru.

The loops may be attached in a variety of ways..... in a seam, knotted and sewn to the surface, or possibly as the loop on the end of a frog.

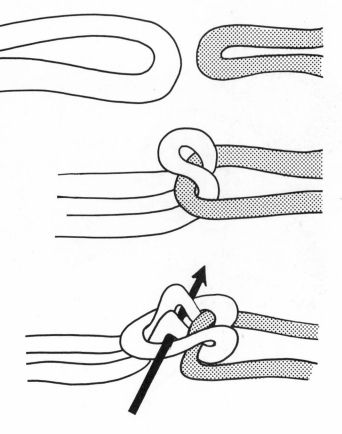

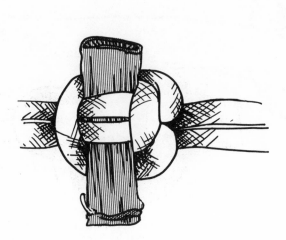

Knotted Ties

Two knots, called hackamores, were originally used to join bands on bridles. These old California cowboy knots can be easily adapted to beautiful ties. If you make them of fabric, make a buttonhole where the slit is indicated.

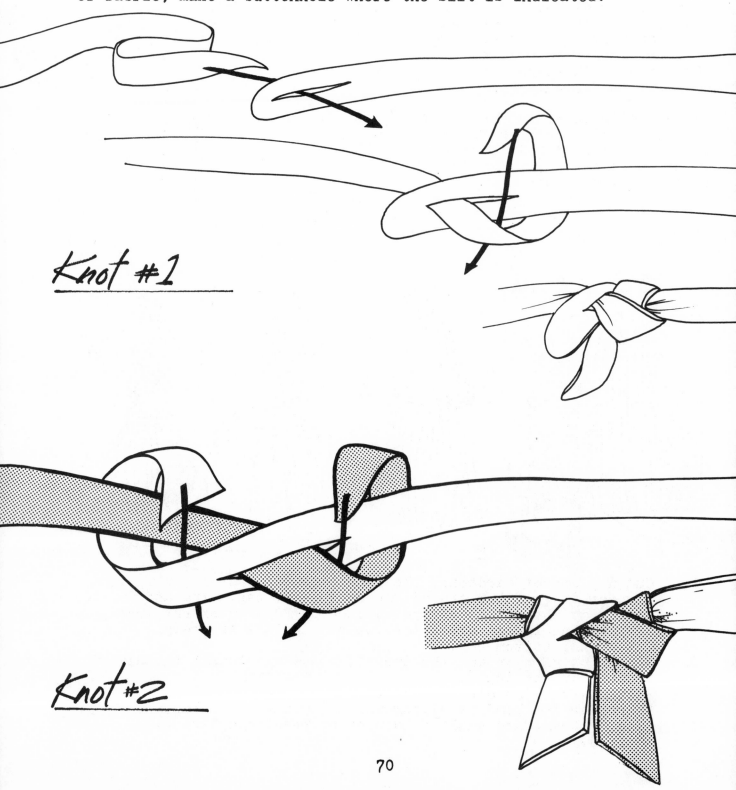

Knot #1

Knot #2

Tassels

Ornaments in the form of tassels have been used for centuries on costumes all over the world. The tassels can be the method of fastening a garment, the end of a tie, or simply the surface decoration with a snap underneath to fasten.

Various effects can be achieved by the materials chosen for the tassel: yarns of all descriptions, soft string, silky threads textured fibers, etc.

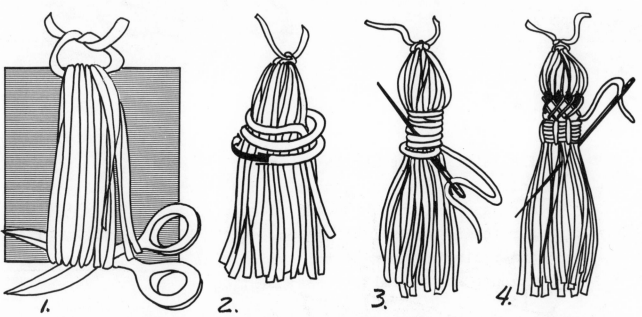

1. Cut a piece of cardboard the length of the tassel. Wrap yarn or other fiber around the cardboard, beginning and ending at the bottom of the cardboard. Cut an extra piece of yarn and insert under the top end and tie securely. Cut at the bottom end.
2. Wrap some yarn around the tassel, about one fourth the distance from the top.
3. Fasten with a needle, as shown.
4. Embroider the band as elaborately as you wish. Pieces of lace, ribbon, and small treasures or beads can also be applied.

Surface Effects

The initial response to an unusual fabric surface normally commands your attention and interest. Exploring and experimenting with the idea of changing the fabric surface is a fascinating one. Working the surfaces of materials,in contrast to working with structural variations, has unlimited possibilities.

Topstitching:

Topstitching is a very easy technique to use for
very professional results. Rows of stitching can
create a tailored effect. From a functionsl stand-
point, topstitching will hold edges and seams flat.
If you need a guide to help keep your rows straight,
line up the edge of the presser foot with the previous row stitched or use the metal guide on your
machine, if you have one.

Special effects:

1. Use many rows of stitching on lightly padded
    areas, i.e. oollars, cuffs...for extra body.
    This idea can also be used to make whole gar-
    ments...vests, for instance....very firm and
    looks terrific.

2. If using a double or triple needle, try two
    or three various shades of thread...nice
    result.

3. To stitch with unusual threads, i.e. metal-
    lic, boucle, or any other threads difficult
    to thread thru the sewing machine needle,
    hand wind, if necessary, onto the bobbin.
    Stitch on the wrong side of your fabric.
    Note: very narrow silky ribbon can also
    be used.

4. Try stitching in a definite pattern. To
    give yourself some guidelines, draw the
    lines to be stitched on the wrong side or
    use a special sewing pen (the lines dis-
    appear) on the right side.

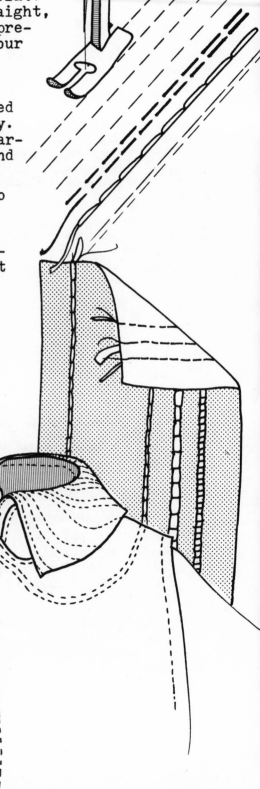

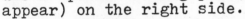

73

Wrinkled & Stitched:

Wrinkles are very often a source or irritation and frustration. These wrinkles, in your fabric of course, can be turned into an innovative design element that can be used in a variety of ways. Natural fibers.. silk, cotton, linen...are the best choices because they naturally wrinkle. The amount of fabric needed depends on how much of a wrinkled effect you want. In general, wrinkling the fabric vertically on the lengthwise grain usually takes up about 1/3 of the width. All over wrinkles that are stitched in all directions can take up as much as 1/2 the fabric in both directions. Plan your yardage accordingly, and note too, that the technique uses a lot of thread

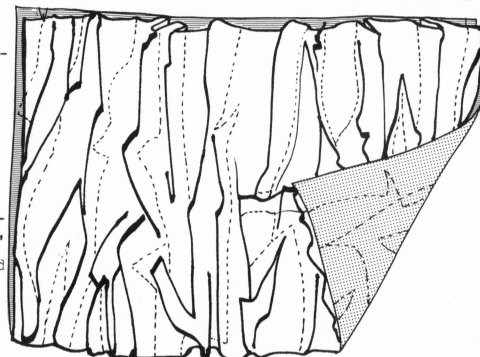

Method:
Wet the fabric, then twist, fold or accordian pleat it. Tie the fabric roll in several places to keep it wrinkled, then let air dry. If is hasn't dried completely after a day or so, untie the fabric very gently and let it continue to air dry.

Meanwhile, cut a piece of underlining fabric several inches larger than the length and width of the pattern pieces. If you don't mind it being a little stiff, Stitch Witchery may be placed between the underlining and the wrinkled fabric to secure while stitching.

When the wrinkled fabric is dry, place on top of the underlining, handling gently so the wrinkles don't fall out. Pin the wrinkled fabric to the underlining, pinning as needed to establish the pattern you will stitch. You may wish to baste instead of pinning or fusing.

Machine stitch along the wrinkles. Stitch as much or as little as you wish, letting the stitching outline the shapes of the wrinkles. There are numerous ways of varying this basic technique for different effects. Try stitching with threads in a contrasting rather than matching colors. Or use a double needle with threads in two nearly matching shades. Corded piping may be added where the wrinkles are large enough to cover the raw edges.

When you finish stitching, cut out your garment.

Mirror Embroidery

Profusely embroidered fabric that incorporates mirrors in the designs is indigenous to the countries of the East. The two examples below show an asymetrical design and one that is very symmetrical.

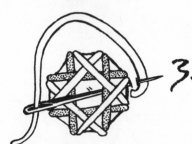

1. Using embroidery thread or perle cotton, take four stitches to make a grid to hold the mirror in place.

2. Take four more stitches, crisscrossing the first four stitches.

3. Make a buttonhole stitch, as shown, by inserting a needle under the basic crossed threads and take up a tiny piece of fabric. Make sure the thread wraps around the needle.

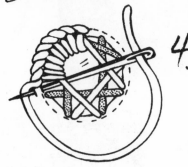

4. Continue around until the edge of the mirror is covered. The cretan stitch can also be used to attach the mirrors. To enrich your designs try a variety of stitches, i.e. chain stitches or French knots. Consider applique to add further interest and color.

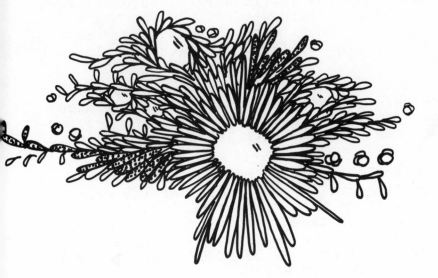

75

Decorative Tacks

These decorative tacks can be used on pockets, points of darts, the inside edges of buttonholes, and the top of pleats or slits.

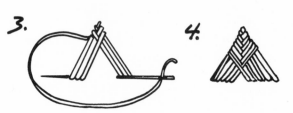

1. Baste a triangle on the fabric. Traditionally these tacks are 1/2" or 5/8". Start the thread at A and take a tiny stitch from right to left at B.

2. Insert needle at C, take a long stitch, emerging to the right of A.

3. & 4. Continue until the tack is filled in.

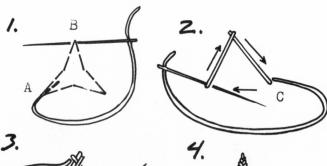

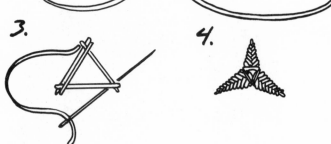

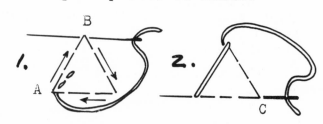

1. This tack starts the same way as the other, baste a triangle on your fabric.

2. Bring the needle up at A and take a very small stitch from right to left at B.

3. Make a small diagonal stitch at C, proceed to A.

4. Take another small stitch... continue around. The stitches will converge toward the center.

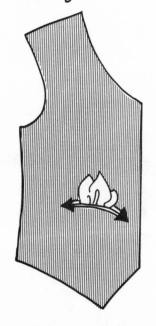

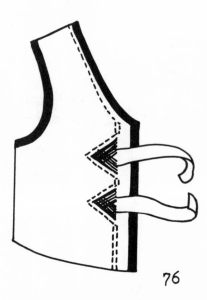

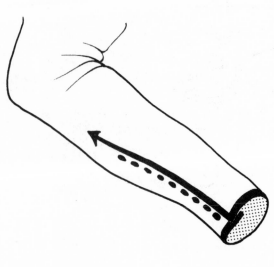

Beading

Various beads, small flat buttons, or short sections of narrow plastic tubing can all be used for beading. The techniques for applying are shown below.

1. The Indians used porcupine quills (cut and flattened) to sew onto garments.
   To achieve this look, narrow plastic tubing can be easily cut with a knife or scissors to the desired length. Tubular glass beads can also be used when a more elegant effect is desired. Slide the tube onto the needle. Take a small stitch in the fabric, add another bead.

2. Simply stitching the beads to the fabric.

3. Use small flat buttons or sequin-like beads with a small bead sewn in the center to fasten.

4. Slide bead on the thread, take a short back stitch to fasten. Add next bead.

5. Thread the beads on a strand of embroidery floss, or other thread. Take a stitch over this strand between each bead. A knotted stitch could also be used as a spacer and as a way to tack the strand in place.

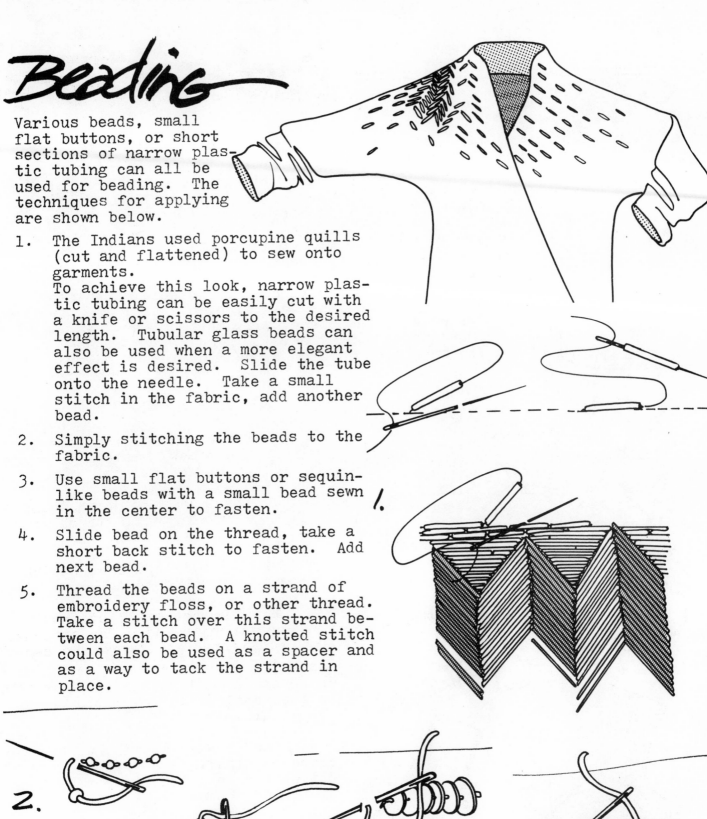

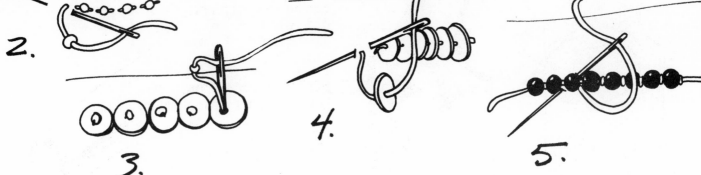

Applique

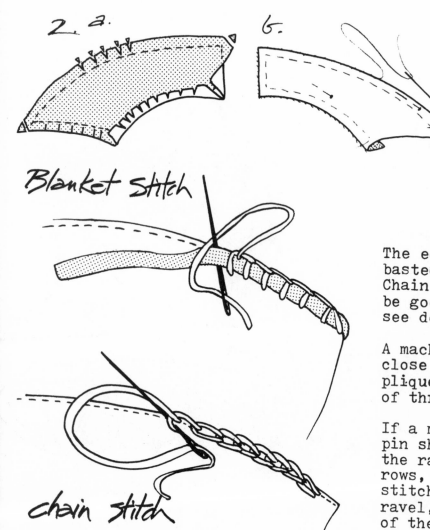

Applique is a good technique for use with small treasures, pieces of painted fabric or stenciled materials, in addition to pieces from your scrap box.

Applique can be combined effectively with patchwork and embroidery...also with many of the other methods in this book.

1. Straight pieces of fabric are simple to apply...the first seam can be sewn on by machine. Fold over, turn the edges under, press...then machine or hand stitch.

2.a. Curved and rounded pieces need special treatment. Baste a line at the fold line, at least 1/4" in from the edge of the piece, slip to the line.

   b. Press on basting line.

   c. Pin in place. Stitch by hand or top stitch by machine

Blanket Stitch

chain stitch

The edges of appliqued pieces can be basted in place and embroidered. Chain or blanket stitches would both be good choices to cover the edges, see detail.

A machine zig-zag stitch, worked very close together, is a great way to applique...this method does take a <u>lot</u> of thread, however.

If a more casual look is desired, pin shapes to the fabric and leave the raw edges showing. Stitch two rows, close together, using 8-10 stitches per inch. The edges will ravel, an effect that will be part of the design.

We most often use pieces of fabric
for applique, however, this technique can have many interpretations.

Ideas: Sections of braided or
plaited tubes outlined
with ribbon or lace

Cut-outs of non-ravelling
materials...i.e. leather,
leather-like fabric, felt,
or melton wool....placed
over a constrasting color
to show thru the cut-out,
top stitch

Small fabric pieces, em-
broidered...cover the raw
edges with cording, fabric
tubes or bias strips

Bias bands arranged in a
geometric design

If the pieces to be appliqued are sheer,
ravel easily or are an intricate shape...
you may wish to cut a 'facing' of another
material.

1. Pin pieces right sides together
2. Stitch around, leaving a small
    opening. Clip.
3. Turn thru opening, slip stitch
    closed, press. Hand stitch in
    place.

Ribbon Embroidery

Ribbon embroidery is a very
traditional technique that can be
used effectively in a contemporary way.
Plant forms of all descriptions can easily
be adapted to this type of decoration. Geometric
designs or intricate medallions would also be possibilities. Ribbon embroidery is easily executed on a
very loosely woven fabric, also on knits or crocheted
garments.

Method:

Use a large-eyed sharp needle.
Try using a variety of sizes
and textures of ribbon. The
silky, smooth ones will be
easier to pull thru the fabric.
As you sew with the ribbon you
may wish to try twisting or
knotting the ribbon for an
interesting effect.

1.

2.

3.

As you work with the ribbon,
you will probably see areas
to embellish with stitches of
embroidery thread, perle cotton
or silk floss. This decoration
can unify the separate design
elements.

To miter ribbon to fit a
corner: fold ribbon on the
horizontal dotted line.
Stitch on the diagonal line...
or tie an overhand knot.
Press out flat and stitch
in place.

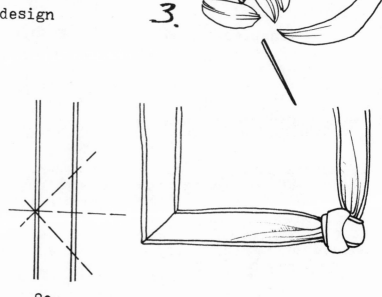

Weaving, using strips of material or ribbon, is another method of changing the surfaces of your fabric. One definite plus for choosing ribbon is the edges are finished. This detailing could be used on pockets, yokes, evening bags, belts or whole garments.

If you plan to use fabric strips, see the how-to on page 50.
Method: Cut a piece of cardboard slightly larger than the part of the garment to be made. Cut the pattern pieces from the main or most predominant color, so if it happens to show between the weaving, the colors will blend in. At the top, pin the warp (lengthwise strips) to these cut-out pieces...placing the strips close together. If the whole piece is to be covered, then place the warp all the way across. The warp can be placed vertically or diagonally.

Weave over and under the warp with the extra strips (the weft), arranging the colors and/or patterns artistically. Pin the beginning and end of each weft as it is woven, weaving strips very close together. Continue until the designated space has been filled. Machine or hand baste, fastening the warp and weft end to the lining... remove the pins. Finish the garment.

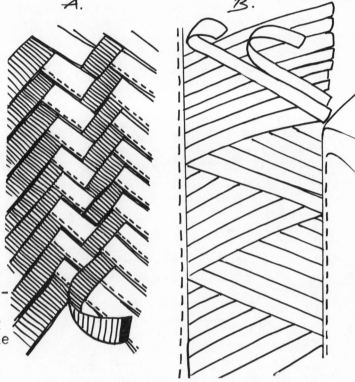

Placing the strips on the diagonal will give the effect as in diagram A.

If the space to be filled is narrow, as in example B, this would be a good method to try. Cut strips the desired length. Place 6 or 8 strips over these, as shown. When finished, cover ends with a facing or patchwork strip. Topstitch.

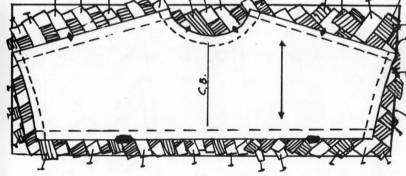

If only a part of a garment is woven, the weft ends need to be finished. In this case the weft ends have been covered with a plain fabric and machine quilted. Another possibility would be to use strip patchwork to cover the weft ends and fill in the space to the edge of the pattern piece. This would also add body to the garment and balance the density of the woven panels. The outer edges of the garment can be faced or bound with bias.

Hopi Braid

The Hopi Indians made wedding sashes with this particular technique. We found that a pliable material, i.e. bias tubes, thick yarns, strips of knit fabric, gives good results. Other possibilities are ribbon, tubing, covered cording, cut strips of fabric or soft leather.

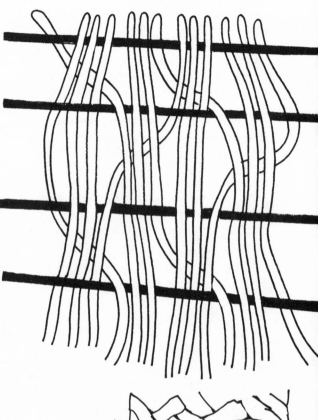

The "take-up" (the length used at the technique progresses) is very little, so on a project where the finished length for example, is 15", cut strips 20". The number of strips needed is an even number, divisable by 6, plus one extra strip.
You will need 4 <u>smooth</u> flat sticks slightly longer than the width of your finished piece. Note: it is important to keep the strips in order as you work...mistakes are easy to see (later) but almost impossible to fix when you are 2 or more rows past them. Use a larkshead or 'price tag' knot if your strips are long enough to fold in half...or tie, sew or pin the strips to one stick. Clamp or secure this stick to a table.

Method:
Starting on the right-hand side, use one stick...pick up the first strip...*slide it under the next 3 strips. Place these first 3 strips under the stick. Pick up that one that travelled under...place it on top of the stick together with the next 2 strips.* This is the basic method, alternate beginning from one side to the other. Repeat between the asterisks (*), starting on the left side, by picking up the next strip and sliding it under the next 3.
At the end of each row, you will have one extra strip to start the next row. Leave the stick in place on the first row, start the next row with a new stick. After you have used the 3 sticks, slide the first one out to use on the next row and tighten your work by pushing up, towards the top, with the next stick.

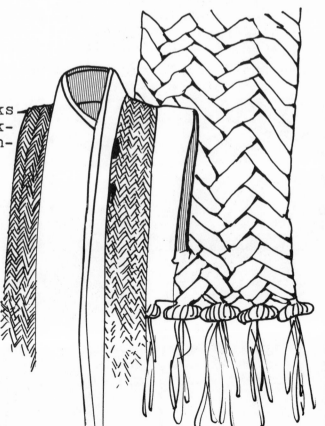

Weaving in fabric

This project is a simple introduction to weaving. Slashed fabric has taken the place of string or thread for the warp. The wefts are the crosswise elements. These could be textured fibers, ribbon, yarn, leather or narrow strips of fabric that would add interest. The outer form of the weaving can be most any shape. Consideration: simple shapes are easiest...at least for the first effort.

1. Choose fabric that is closely woven for the background. On the wrong side of the fabric...draw a line the shape of the section to be woven. Cut slashes about 3/8" apart, lengthwise in that shape. Pin to a piece of cardboard.

2. Thread yarn needle with a strip of fabric, or other fiber. Slide needle over and under the 'warps' across the row. The next row will use the opposite 'warps'. The ends of these horizontal elements need not be fastened...each beginning and ending can show from the front and be a part of the design. for added interest knot these ends. Pack the rows tightly with the needle or a table fork.

3. Add a reinforcing piece to the back of the garment.

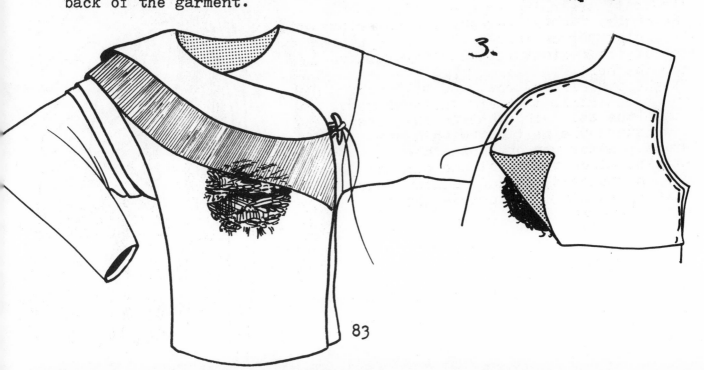

Tucks n' Pleats

To eliminate tedious marking of tucks and pleats for your garments... simply sew those tucks on your machine before you cut the fabric. In the case of pleats, pin or baste and lightly press in place, then cut your garment.

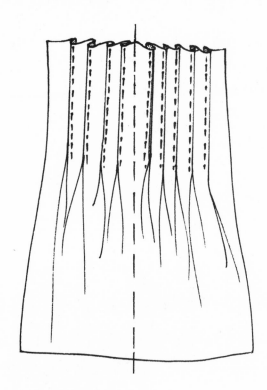

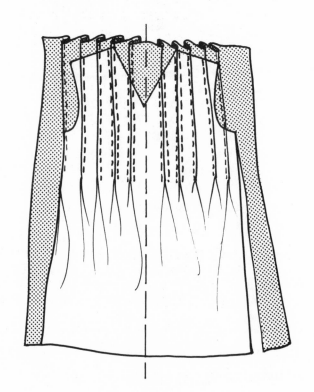

Cut the fabric the length of the pattern piece to be tucked or pleated.

Run a basting line on the center of the fabric.

Stitch the tucks whatever width you wish (in the case of pleats, pin or baste in place and press).

Pin pattern pieces to the fabric, matching the center with the basting line.

Cut out pieces and proceed with the garment.

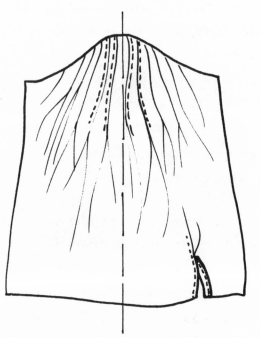

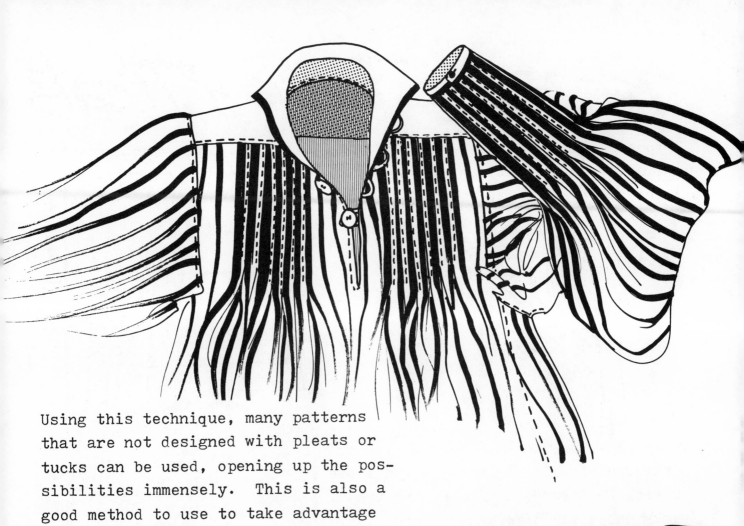

Using this technique, many patterns
that are not designed with pleats or
tucks can be used, opening up the possibilities immensely. This is also a
good method to use to take advantage
of stripes...making one color more predominant, perhaps.
Instead of topstitching pleats in
place, you may wish to add interest
at the top of the pleated section with
embroidery. Repeated rows of a stitch
can be very effective, cross stitch,
for example. If the pleats are very
narrow, smocking would be a good choice.

Making tucks on a definite, bold print
or stripe can improve the design.

To show the difference you may wish to
make a companion garment, using the
fabric in its original state.
To carry out the crisp effect of the
print, you may want to try topstitching the tucks.

Pin Tucks

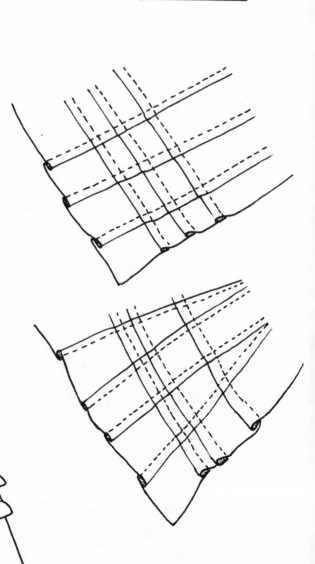

Tucks are a way to emphasize a line or a styling detail. In addition to those already mentioned, pin tucks are probably the easiest to make. These very narrow tucks are made by creasing the fabric along the grain line where you want the tuck. Stitch 1/8" from the fold. Note: to ensure evenly spaced tucks, a notched cardboard guide may be helpful. Use your guide or the presser-foot on your machine to measure the next tuck.

Consider arranging the tucks in groups as well as evenly spacing them. Cross tucking is another possibility. First make all the vertical tucks, then cross them with the horizontal ones.

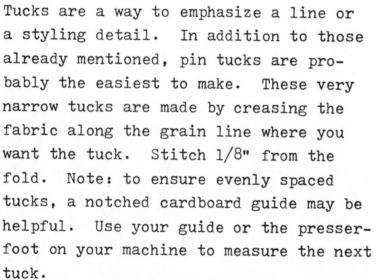

...As Dart Equivalants.

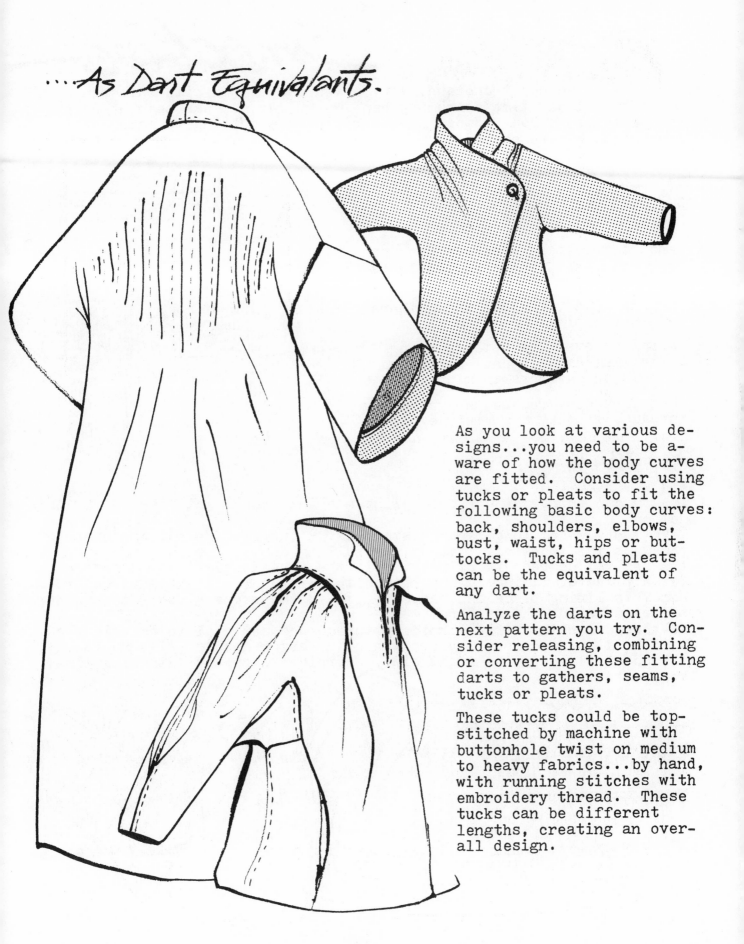

As you look at various designs...you need to be aware of how the body curves are fitted. Consider using tucks or pleats to fit the following basic body curves: back, shoulders, elbows, bust, waist, hips or buttocks. Tucks and pleats can be the equivalent of any dart.

Analyze the darts on the next pattern you try. Consider releasing, combining or converting these fitting darts to gathers, seams, tucks or pleats.

These tucks could be topstitched by machine with buttonhole twist on medium to heavy fabrics...by hand, with running stitches with embroidery thread. These tucks can be different lengths, creating an overall design.

87

Smocking

Smocking is an old technique, very often associated with children's clothes. It was time-consuming hand work that now has been up-dated in usage and method. Smock the fabric before cutting to make the garment size more correct.

By Hand:

1. Hand baste, using evenly spaced running stitches. The rows should be about 1/4" apart.

2. Pull threads to adjust the gathers and fasten.

3. Embroider over the gathers using horizontal and diagonal stitching to hold the gathers in place.

   When finished, remove the gathering threads, if they are visible.

By Machine:

1. If you can embroider on your sewing machine, you might like to try this method.
   Make two rows of long machine stitches, $\frac{1}{4}$" apart...repeat wherever you want the smocking. Gather, by pulling on the bobbin threads, to the desired degree of fullness. Tie the threads together to fasten.

2. Cut a piece of lining 1" wider than the width of all the gathered rows. Hem this lining piece and baste or pin to the wrong side of the gathered piece, covering the gathers.

3. Re-thread machine with embroidery thread and set dial to embroider a stitch of your choice... you may need a larger needle (#14) so it will thread easily. On the right side, embroider over the gathering line, remove basting.

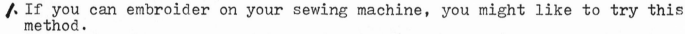

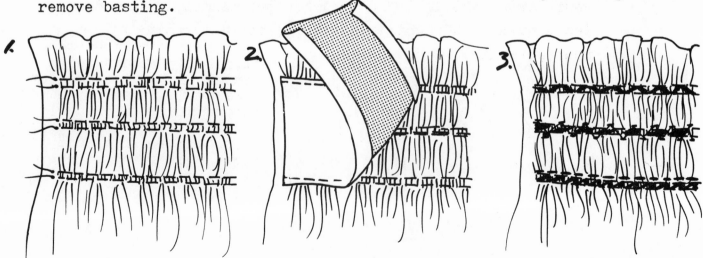

Construction Details

In addition to decorating the surface of the fabric....
many other methods can be used to change the appearance
of the material and make your garment unique. The techniques in this chapter will be important ones to add to
your sewing skills. When you are proficient at these
techniques, you might even welcome close scrutiny of
your garments.

Seam finishes

Most fabrics need some kind of seam finishing, especially on fabrics that ravel. When the garment you make is very special and unique... finishing the seams is almost demanded, if the garment isn't lined.

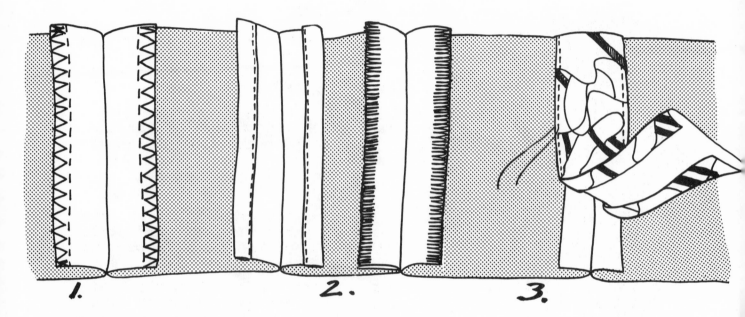

1.

2.

3.

1. Pinking or zig-zagging seams (fig. 1) are two very basic seam finishes. Binding the seams with commercial bias tape can be done on each individual piece of the garment (fig. 2), or after the seams are sewn together...then the edges are bound as one.

2. Overcasting the seams by hand or machine (fig. 3) or covering the seam with a strip of fabric (fig. 4) would also be possibilities.

    The following is another method that uses a contrasting strip of fabric to cover the seams on the <u>outside</u> of your garment. This is a good way to add interest or to camouflage uneven patchwork.

    Cut strips the length of the seams to be covered. The width can vary, 1½" to 2" would be average. If the seams are straight, cut the fabric on the straight...if curved, use bias strips.

3. With the wrong sides of the garment together, place one fabric strip on top of the garment. Pin the three layers together. Then stitch on the seam allowance. If the fabric is bulky, grade the seams (trim at different levels so they don't end in exactly the same place). Press band towards seam. Turn the edge of the band under and pin. Topstitch or hand sew in place.

Bulky Seam Finish

This is an easy method to use to finish seams and eliminate bulk. The technique is especially effective with quilted materials, thick woolens like melton, or when dealing with layers of fabric.

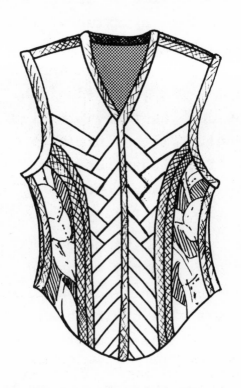

Method:

1. Cut off the seam allowance on the seams to be joined with the bias. Cut a bias strip 1½" - 2" wide and as long as the pieces to be sewn.

2. Stitch the right side of the bias to the right side of the garment pieces, ¼" to ½" from the edge...depending on how much of the bias trim you want to show.

3. Place the right sides of both pattern pieces together and stitch the bias only. This will be sewn at the original seam line.

4. On the inside, turn the bias under and stitch by hand to finish these edges. Finish outside seams last, see page 92.

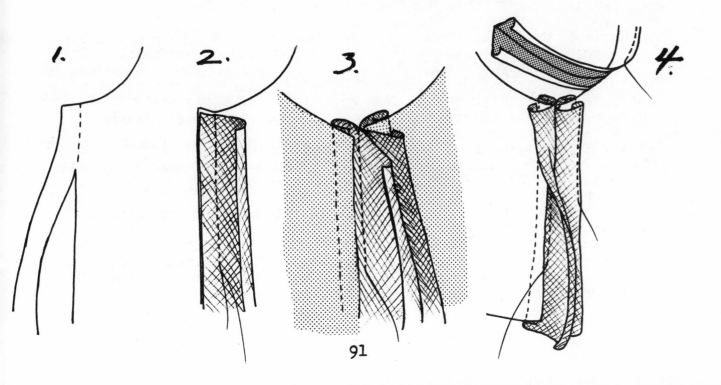

Bias finish

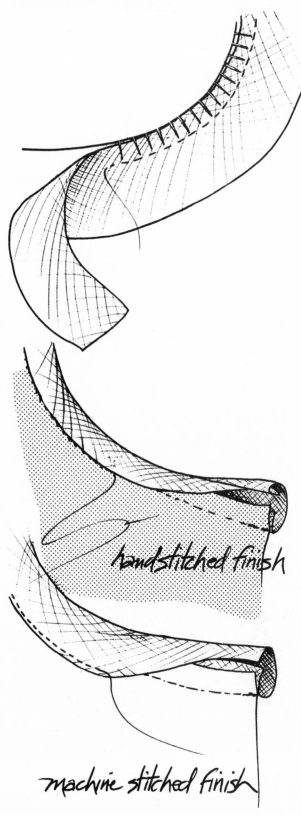

handstitched finish

machine stitched finish

Consider using a bias binding to finish an edge or replace a facing. This bias, in addition to a matching fabric, could also be cut of a constrasting color or texture. If the bias is to show as a trim, cut off the seam allowance. Cut the bias four times the finished width. With right sides together, pin bias to the garment. Stitch in place. Clip curves if necessary or trim the seams, if desired. Turn to wrong side...handstitch in place.

If there is topstitching somewhere on your garment, you may wish to topstitch the bias trim. If so, place the right side of the bias on the wrong side of the garment. Pin and stitch, as above. Turn under bias strip on the outside. Topstitch.

Note: if the bias is to replace a facing and will not be showing...do not trim off the seam allowance. After stitching the bias at the indicated seam allowance, clip seams. Press seam allowance towards bias, grading seams if necessary. Stitch, as shown, to roll under. Turn under raw edge and handstitch in place.

Flat felled Seam:

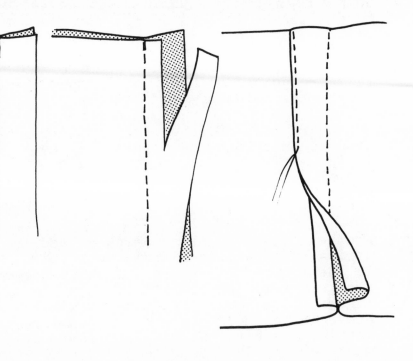

Flat felled seams are ex-
cellent as a finish, one
that looks very tailored.
This technique is often
used to finish the seams
on a man's shirt.
With the wrong sides to-
gether, stitch seam so
the seam is on the out-
side. Trim <u>one</u> side of
the seam close to the
stitching (1/8"). Fold
the remaining edge over
the trimmed edge, stitch
again. Press.

French seam finishes are used for most fine fabrics, especially
if minimal seam allowances are required. The seams are very
narrow, also stitched twice, so it is strong and the raw edge is
enclosed. This type of seam finish is used on fine lingerie.

French Seam:

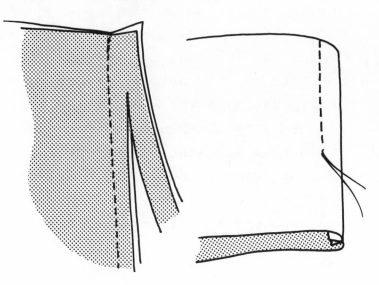

With the wrong sides together,
stitch seams 1/8" from edge.
The first seam will be on the
right side. Press all one
direction. Trim if necessary
and turn to the wrong side.
Stitch the balance of the
seam allowance. The seam is
now enclosed.
Note: if it is difficult to
sew the first seam 1/8", sew
it with a wider seam allowance and trim it to 1/8".

Decorative Seam Joinings

Many cultures use a variety of decorative handstitching to join fabric strips. Some stitches are worked very close with the fabrics butted together. In the other technique, faggoting, the pieces of material are joined with stitching that allows space between.

There are many stitches that could be used to embroider and decorate a seam. In the example on the right, begin by basting a triangle or other shape on the seams to be covered. Satin stitches are then sewn in a triangle.

Another stitch that is commonly used in Africa and South America to join seams is the figure '8'. This stitch is worked from right to left...left to right in a figure '8'. The alternating stitches cross in the middle of the '8', where the two pieces of fabric join (keep in mind how you lace your shoes).

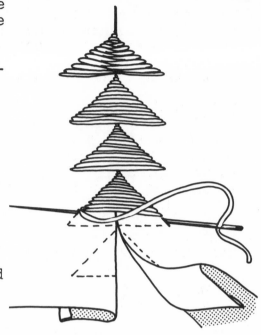

Faggoting Stitches:

Faggoting is a method of joining two pieces of cloth in a decorative way. The knotted insertion stitch (left, below) is made as follows. A small buttonhole stitch is worked on the edge of the material and a second stitch is made over the resulting loop, see diagram.

The Swedish knot stitch (right, below) is worked by bringing the needle up on one edge of the piece to be joined. A long stitch across to the other piece of fabric, bringing the needle up to the right side of the material. Insert needle, as shown, making a knot.

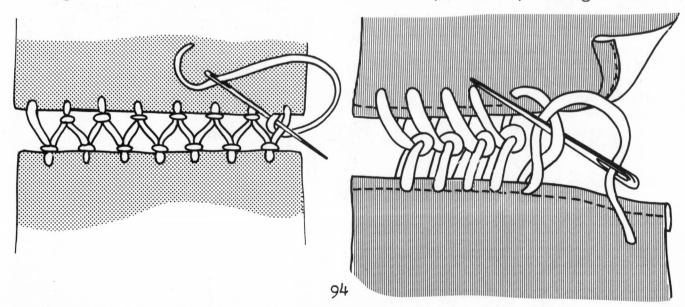

To prepare the fabric for faggoting, hem the two edges of material to be joined. Pin these pieces to a piece of heavy paper to keep them equidistant, as you are sewing.

Twisted Bar

Start the thread underneath at one edge of the material and take one stitch opposite. Take several turns around the bar for a twisted effect. Finish the stitch by inserting the needle at the starting point. Slip the needle along, in the hem, for $\frac{1}{2}$" and then work another twisted bar.

With Beads

To combine beads with the faggoting stitches, use any of the stitches shown and slip a bead on the needle before each stitch.

With Cords or Tapes

Arrange the tapes or cords on the heavy paper and pin in place. Join these together with any of the faggoting stitches illustrated. Beads could be added if desired.

Arrange the tapes or cords on the heavy paper and pin in place. Join these together with any of the faggoting stitches illustrated. Beads could be added if desired.

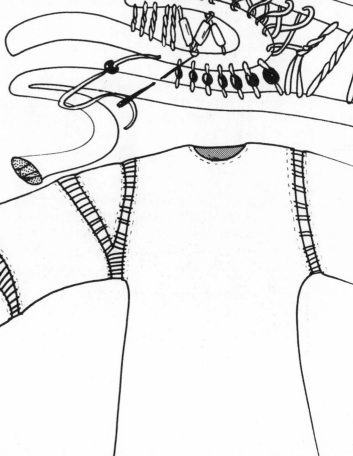

facings & Hems

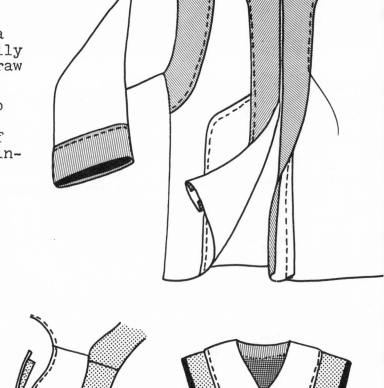

A facing is rarely considered a decorative accent. It is usually a utilitarian way to finish a raw edge.

The facing edge that is sewn to the garment is cut the same as the pattern. The outer edge of the facing could be cut in an interesting shape.

Consider using a facing where none is needed...an armhole facing <u>with</u> sleeves or a neck facing <u>with</u> a collar.

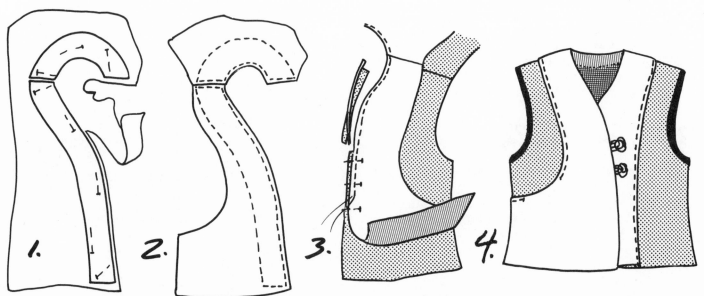

1. First sew the facing pieces together as indicated in the pattern. Press seams open. Place the wrong side of the garment next to the right side of the facing. Pin in place and stitch.

2. Trim ¼" from stitching and clip curves where necessary.

3. Turn to the right side of the garment, then machine or hand stitch the outer edge in place.

4. Press as usual.

Note: Even if you don't cut the outer edges in an unusual shape, you can do the same thing with the regular shape of the facings.

Designing facings & Shaped Hems

Shaped hems and sleeves can be an interesting area to make an individual statement. They could be padded also, if desired. The facing could be a constrasting color or print.

Cut the facing the same length as the piece to be faced. The depth would depend on the width of the shaping. Draw the desired shape on the facing. Pin to the hem of the garment, or to the sleeves. Stitch, trim or clip and turn. Press.

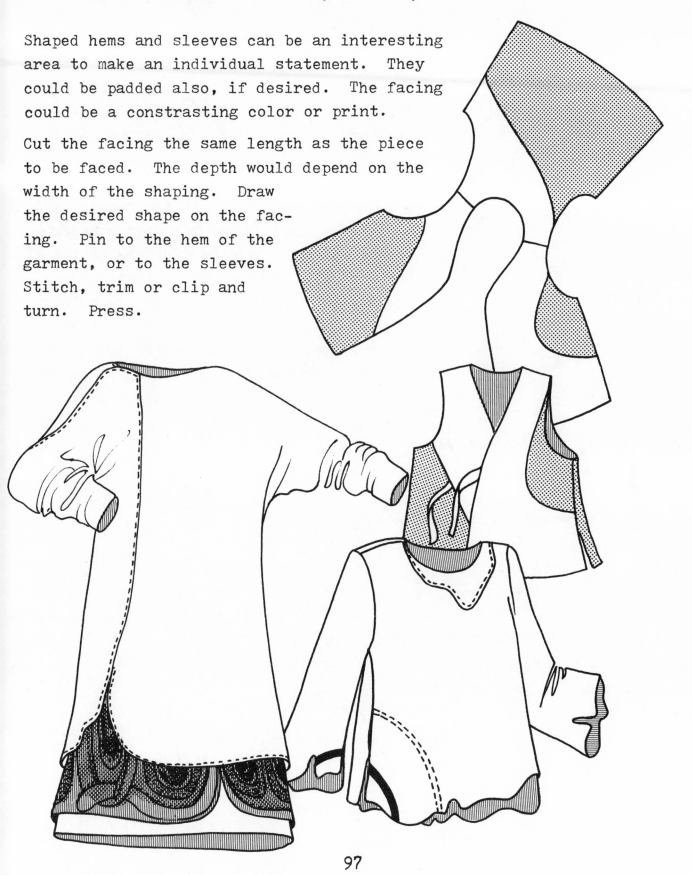

Loose Layering

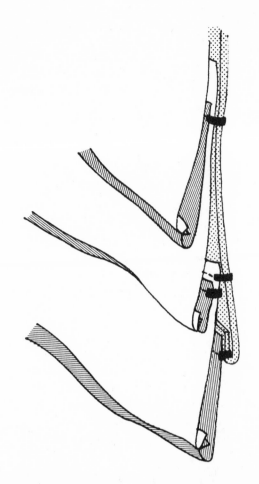

When designing a garment with the layering technique, consider that all of the faced flaps will be loose. The layering should be done with medium to lightweight fabrics for the pieces as well as the lining. The pieces can be sewn to a lining, each piece covering the joining of the previous one. If the garment is not to be lined, that back piece needs to be the shape of the finished pattern piece. The drawing on the left shows a cross section of the layering technique. For easy reference, the black bars indicate graphically which layers are connected. The backing or facing material needs to be cut on the straight grain.

Designing Considerations:

...Do you want the layers to join at the edges of the garment?

...Are the layers going to be contained inside the edges of the piece or will they run thru the edges?

...Will the layers incorporate any other structural aspects of the garment, i.e. pockets, closures, etc.

...Will the lining show along the edge or be completely hidden? When pressing the finished pieces, consider pressing to show a thin or thick line.

...Are you going to line the pieces with a contrasting fabric?

...Will the pieces be cut on the straight grain or on the bias?

...What will overlap and what will be underneath?

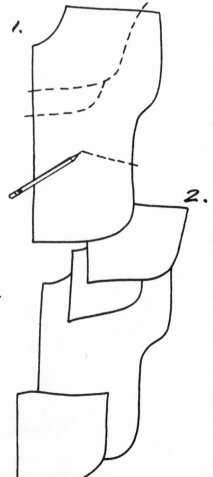

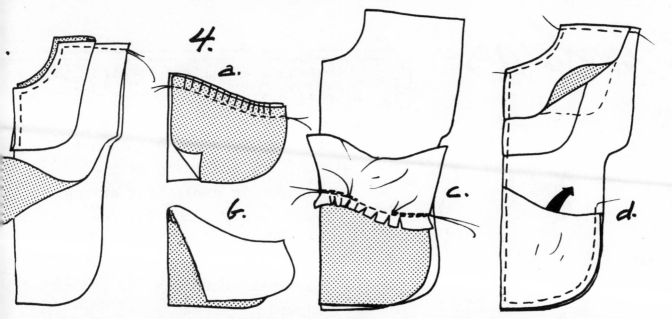

1. Make a copy of the pattern piece you will be layering. Draw the lines indicating the finished shape of the layers. Next, decide how much of each flap will extend and show.

2. Make a paper paper pattern for each piece to be cut. Add seam allowances and cut out pieces and a lining for each. Grain lines should be constant.

3. Stitch each section, right sides together, leaving the top edge open. Clip, grade seams and turn. Press. Starting with the deepest layer, fasten the first piece to the lining, if one is used. Continue to fill in the space, overlapping the faced pieces. If no lining is used, stack layers on top of each other, starting with the longest one...ending with the shortest one.

4. To incorporate a pocket in the layering...stitch a lining to a pocket piece along top edge of the pocket, see A. Stitch and clip. B. Turn and press. C. Attach the pocket to the backing piece by stitching in between the lining and the pocket piece along the previous seam line. D. Baste the edges of the pocket to the backing piece.

5. Baste the raw edges along the seam lines. Note: all pieces will not necessarily extend to the seam allowance. Some may be finished on three sides, connecting at the top.

6. Finish the edges with binding (A), facings or linings (B).

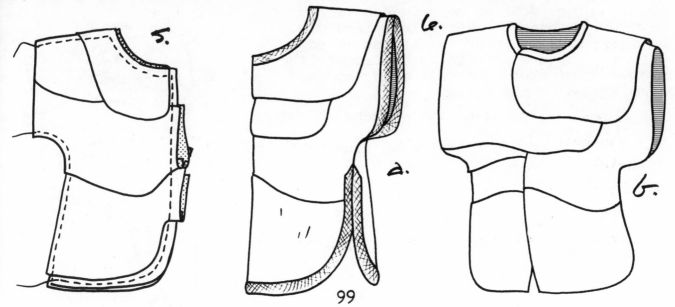

Windows

'Windows' are one way to highlight
a textile treasure or other small
piece to make it more important.
If you wish to make more than one
'window' try combining similar
shapes in a pleasing arrange-
ment. Try using this concept
on children's clothes. Use one
of their drawings translated
into an embroidery or printed
fabric.

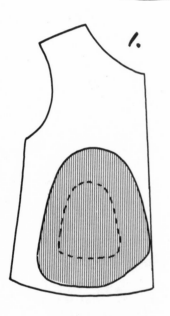

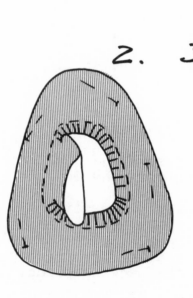

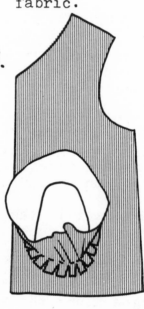

Method:

Cut a facing, four or more inches larger
than the 'window'. The facing piece may
be a contrasting color, a very small edge
will show when it is finished...looks like
piping. For each 'window', draw the desired shape on the facing.

1. Place the facing on the garment, right
   sides together.
2. Pin to secure and stitch on line made
   on the facing. Cut close, clip curves
   or corners.
3. Turn and press.
4. Place the piece you wish to show behind
   the 'window'. To secure, topstitch the
   opening all around or fasten by hand
   sewing.

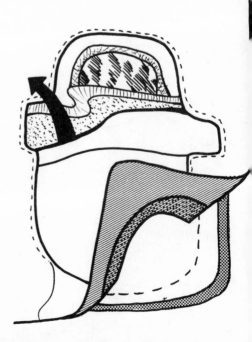

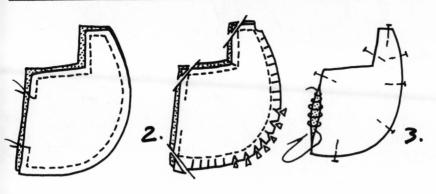

2.   **3.**

Patch-Shaped Pockets:

If a particular shaped pocket is desired, cut a paper pattern to determine the size and shape.

1. Cut two layers of fabric and one layer of interfacing, if necessary. Place right sides of fabric together, lay interfacing on top. Pin.

2. Stitch, leaving one small straight section open. Clip, trim and turn thru small opening.

3. Press. Then whipstitch together.

4. Stitch to garment.

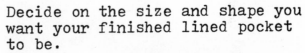

4.

Lined Pocket

Decide on the size and shape you want your finished lined pocket to be.

1. Cut out pocket, adding 1½" hem at the top of the pocket. Cut the lining ½" smaller at the top, than the finished pocket. Add seam allowances all around to both pieces.

2. With the right sides together, stitch the lining and the pocket together at the top edge, leaving a 2" opening in the center.

3. Grade seams if bulky, then press seam down. Fold the pocket as shown and stitch the lining and the pocket together. Clip and trim seam.

4. Turn thru opening. Press. Stitch opening closed and pocket is ready for application.

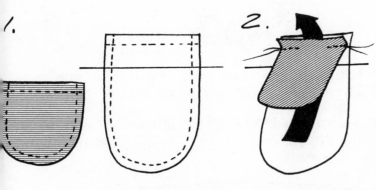

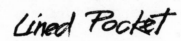

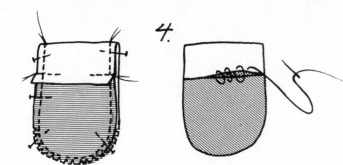

In-Seam Pockets:

To make a shaped opening for an in-seam pocket, first decide how big the pocket is to be and cut two pieces of fabric adding the seam allowances. Both could be contrasting to the garment or just the one that turns back to show the very edge of another color.

1. Place the right side of the pocket to the right side of the front of the garment, as shown. Pin and stitch in the chosen shape.

2. Trim and clip seam. Turn and press.

3. Top stitch for a tailored effect. Place the other pocket piece underneath the facing, matching side seams. Sew the pocket together.

4. Continue with the garment, treating this section just completed as one surface.

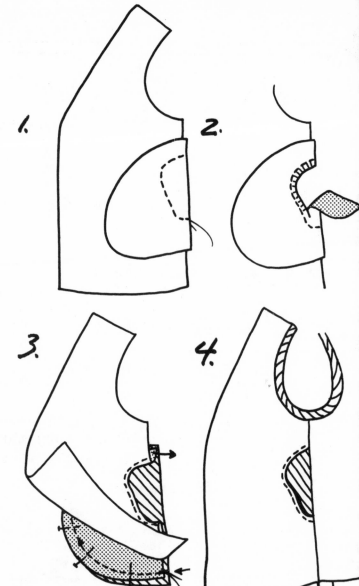

Various ideas, shown below, combine in-seam pockets with techniques in this book. You will probably be able to think of others, too.
A...ribbon inserts B...shaped hole with a knot button closure
C...strip patchwork insert D...printed lining E...Stitched seams with ties

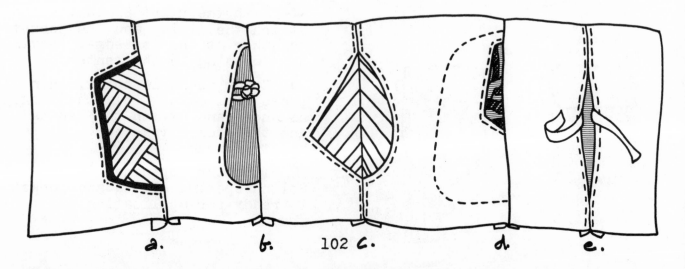

a.　　　　b.　　102 c.　　　　d.　　　e.

Inset Pockets:

These pockets are made using the concept of the window, see page 100. Nice tailored feature for a jacket or a vest, also works well on the outside of a purse for a sunglass 'case'.

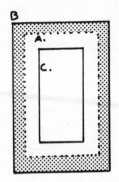

A = finished seam line
B = cutting line for pocket and pocket lining
C = cutting line for the hole in the garment

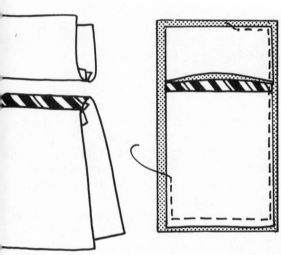

The pocket pieces to be inserted in the window would be cut to fit space 'B'. Two pieces, stitched together, or one long piece folded in half, would be cut for this space. This application looks best if the bottom half is a little larger than the top half.

Trim, if desired. Stitch these two pieces to the interfaced pocket back piece 'B'.

Interfacing is usually required, for most fabrics, on the garment where the hole is to be cut and on the back piece for the pocket, 'B'. Use iron-on interfacing when it is compatible with the material.

1. Stitch on line 'A'. Cut out hole 'C'. Clip carefully to the exact corners.
2. Place pocket back, with the inserts stitched on it, behind the hole, pin in place. Stitch first side, as shown.
3. Continue stitching each side, press.
4. Finished. Topstitching is optional.
   Note: Pockets can be <u>any</u> shape.

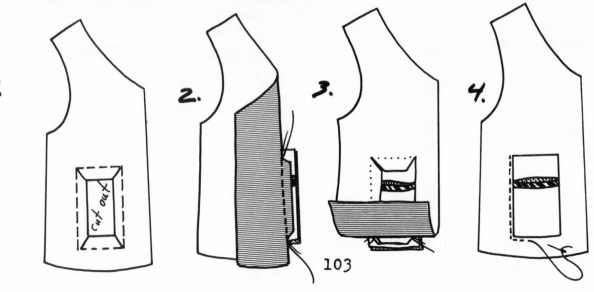

Buttonhole Pocket:

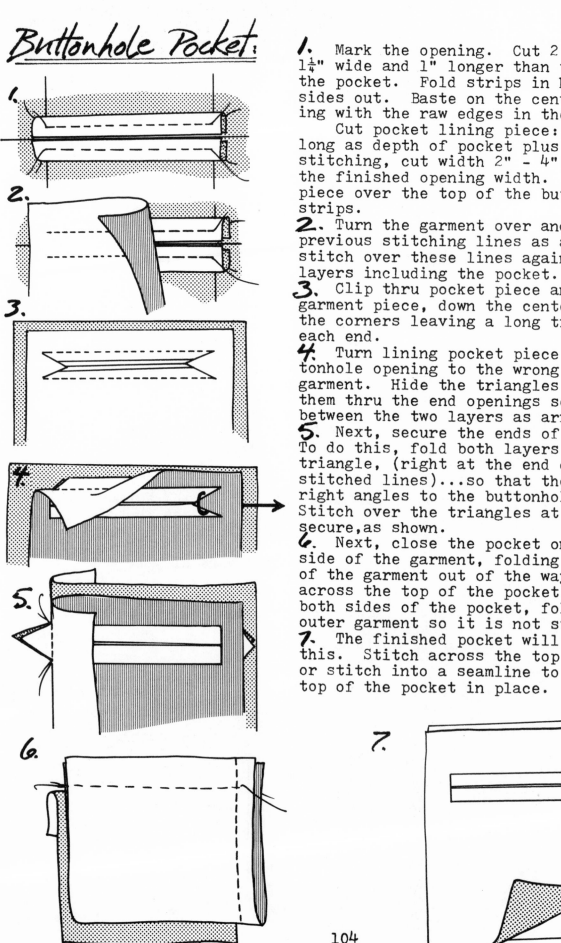

1. Mark the opening. Cut 2 bias strips 1¼" wide and 1" longer than the width of the pocket. Fold strips in half, right sides out. Baste on the center of marking with the raw edges in the center.

Cut pocket lining piece: twice as long as depth of pocket plus 5" for stitching, cut width 2" - 4" wider than the finished opening width. Pin pocket piece over the top of the buttonhole strips.

2. Turn the garment over and using the previous stitching lines as a guide, stitch over these lines again, thru all layers including the pocket.

3. Clip thru pocket piece and outside garment piece, down the center and to the corners leaving a long triangle at each end.

4. Turn lining pocket piece thru the buttonhole opening to the wrong side of the garment. Hide the triangles by pulling them thru the end openings so they are in between the two layers as arrow indicates.

5. Next, secure the ends of the opening. To do this, fold both layers away from the triangle, (right at the end of the side stitched lines)...so that the fold is at right angles to the buttonhole opening. Stitch over the triangles at the fold to secure, as shown.

6. Next, close the pocket on the wrong side of the garment, folding the outside of the garment out of the way, stitch across the top of the pocket. Repeat on both sides of the pocket, folding the outer garment so it is not stitched in.

7. The finished pocket will look like this. Stitch across the top if desired or stitch into a seamline to hold the top of the pocket in place.

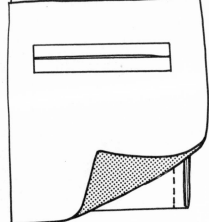

SLEEVES

Unusual sleeve treatments can be the focal point of an entire garment. Often, only minor changes need to be made in the sleeve pattern to yield unique results. When designing a sleeve some considerations might be ▶ the shape of the sleeve
   ▶ the shape of the cuff
   ▶ the techniques to include, i.e. ruffles,
      binding, piping, lace inserts
   ▶ the closure

Below are illustrated just a few of the many possibilities for your consideration.

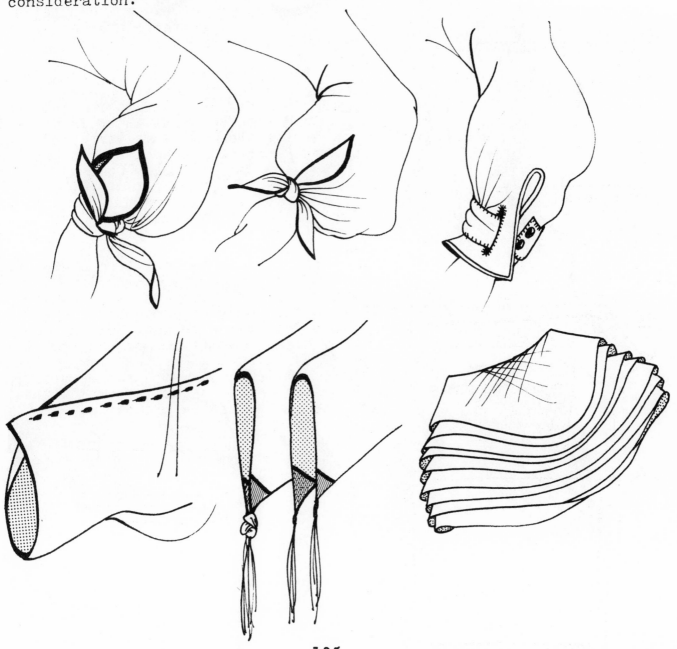

Sleeve Design #1

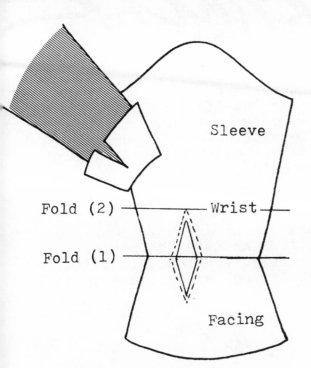

How to make a sleeve with a fold up split cuff.

Make a sleeve facing pattern, as shown. Pin the facing to the sleeve pattern, on the seam allowance. Cut sleeve and facing all together. Mark the dart to line up with the outside wrist. Stitch and clip. Fold on the fold line (1). Turn up cuff (2).

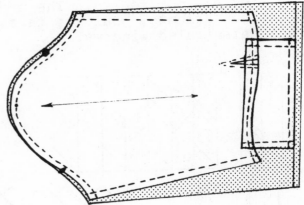

Sleeve Design #2

Design your own tucked cuff. Take a sleeve and cuff pattern, overlap the seam allowances. Place them on a larger piece of paper. Draw the lines straight down both sides of the sleeves, as shown. Add seam allowance at the wrist edge.

To make a new cuff facing pattern:
Measure:...wrist (a)
> ...length of desired facing (b), this would be the length of the tucks at the wrist
> ...circumference of your arm at the point where the tucks end (c)

Draw a rectangle using measurements a and b. Add ½" to lower curve. Subtract ½" from top curve, as shown. Add a ½" to 1" extension on the side to lap when buttoned.

Make tucks on sleeve. Cut facings. Make buttonloops, if desired. Space buttonloops evenly and pin between the tucked sleeve and the cuff. Stitch together. Trim, turn and press. Sew on buttons.

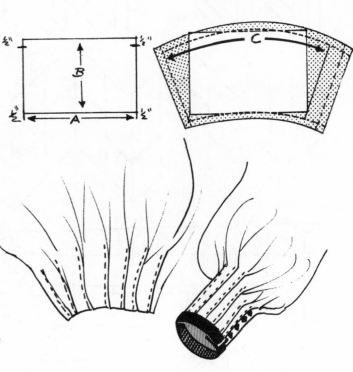

PATCHWORK

Much has been written about traditional patchwork patterns. We will give you a few contemporary ideas. The color combinations you choose can be the key to a very fashionable and up-to-date garment. If a print is used, it will pretty much dictate the 'feeling' of the garment. Color choices are easy to decide, if you relate them to the print. As you become more daring and 'comfortable' with choosing the colors, you may wish to try more unusual color schemes. Interesting textures of fabrics are also a consideration.

Seminole:

Seminole patchwork has an infinite number of pattern possibilities and are the repetition of a single block design. The uses for this technique, in addition to entire garments, could be tabs, pockets, collars, sleeve or bodice insets...also windows.

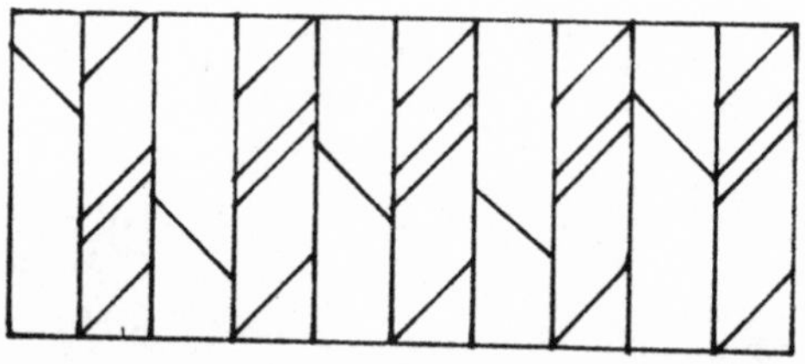

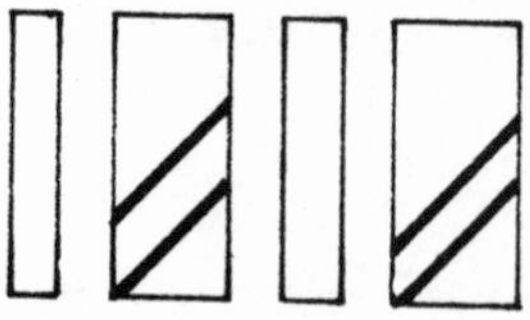

method:

Cut several fabrics into strips, following the lengthwise grain. These strips are sewn together to make a wide strip, see A. Cut up the strip, as shown. The pieces can be cut straight or at an angle. Sew the pieces together to make a band. This is a good technique to use for experimenting with shapes and various color combinations.

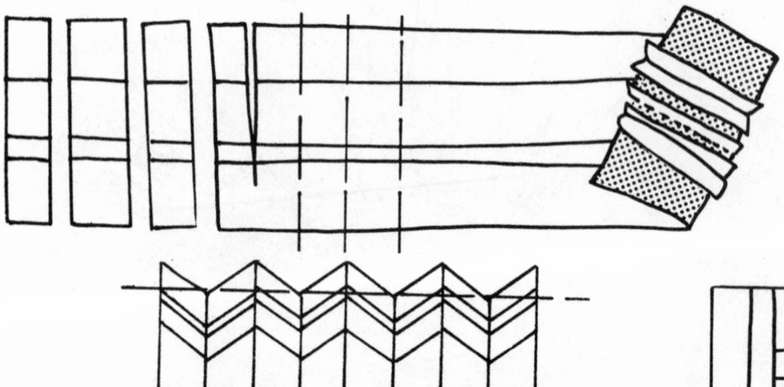

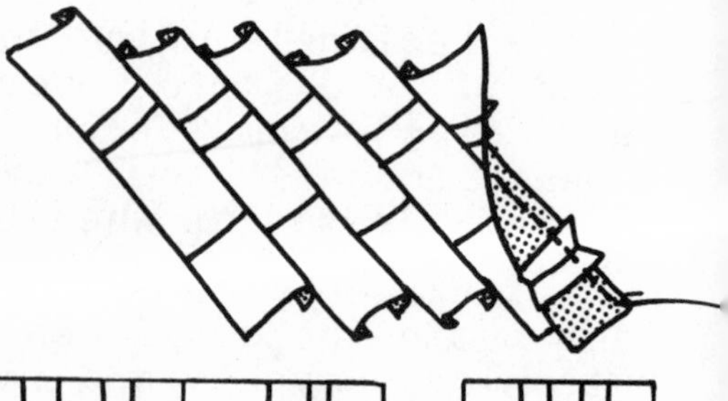

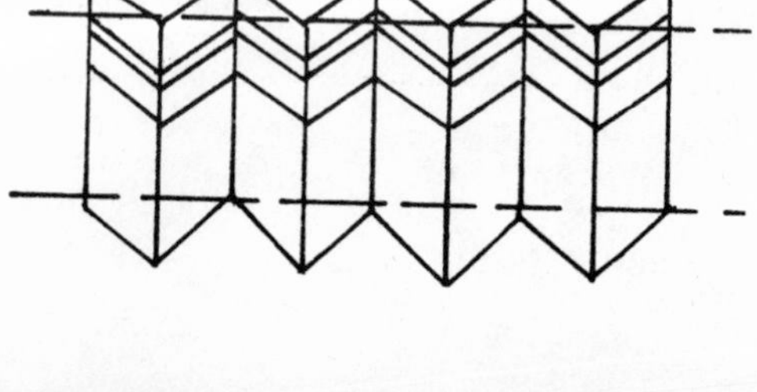

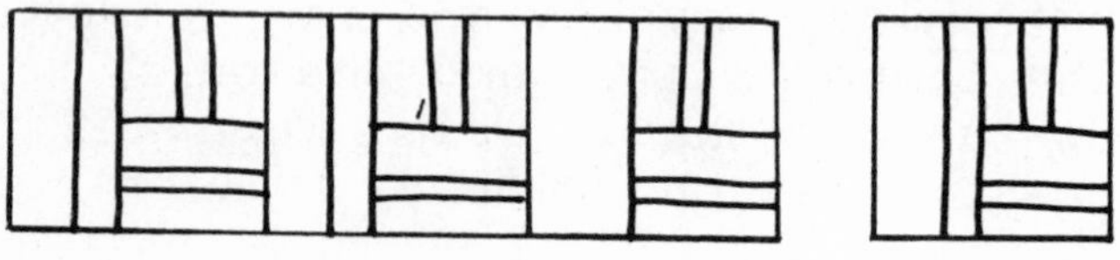

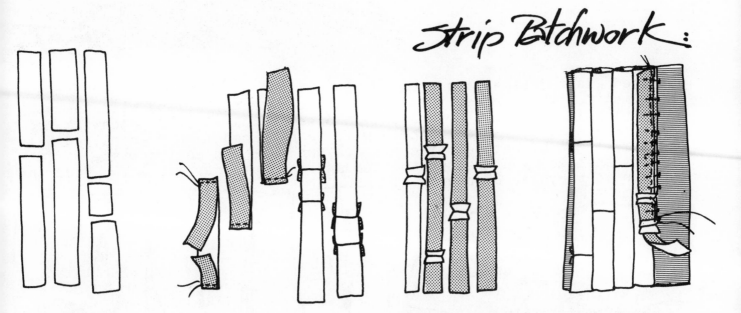

Strip Patchwork:

Method: Cut out the lining fabric, using a simple pattern, preferably one without darts. If the garment is to be quilted, cut the batting the same. Baste these two layers together.

Cut the strips for the patchwork, whatever width you choose...1" to 2½"...the wider the strips, the faster the project. Whole strips can be used or you may wish to piece them, with a definite design in mind.

Sew the pieces together to make the strips, if you are piecing them, press seams open. If you make the decisions on several strips at a time, you can sew and press more than one, it seems to save a little time.

Start at one side or in the middle of the lining piece (front or back). Pin the first strip down on top of the lining (with or without the batting). Take the next sewn strip, place it right side down on top of the first strip. Stitch in place, make sure the piece underneath is included in the seam...it is impossible to fix neatly if it is not remedied immediately. Keep piecing, pressing, and stitching until you've covered the lining.

Finish the garment as usual, covering the seams with bias or other seam finishes...or line the whole garment.

A very definite print, such as a scene, can be cut up and put back together with plain strips of a matching color. These connecting strips can vary in width for interest. Simply cut the print into strips, 2½" to 3" wide and number for easy reassembly. Stitch together with the narrow plain colored fabric. Cut out the garment from this 'yardage' or stitch the strips together on the cut out lining.

Stained glass designs are usually planned as you would a shaped patchwork motif with fabrics. The patchwork can be emphasized with the use of piping in the seams or gradual shading. Look at your patchwork project as a series of blocks which will be combined then re-combined with larger blocks of patched pieces. You can patch an entire piece of fabric, then place your pattern on top and cut out your garment. Save the scraps to recycle, of course.

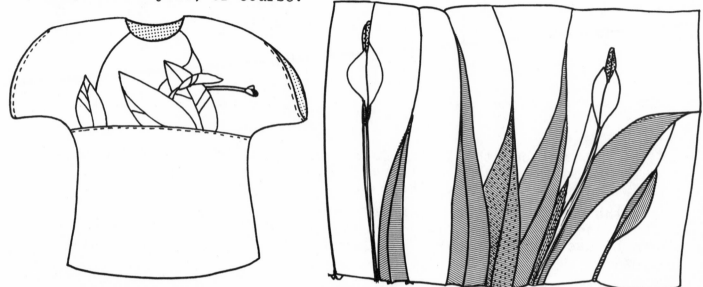

1. Draw the desired shape on the wrong side of the fabric. This first line is the finished seam line. Draw the 2nd line to the inside of that 1st line (seam allowance) which will be the cutting line. Next, cut the piece to be inset, adding an equal seam allowance. Clip all curves, mark the point with a thread or pen. 2. Pin and stitch one side, don't stretch the seams. Grade seams. Press this first seam flat either in or out depending on the finish you want. 3. Working from the front side of your piece, turn the seam allowance under. Lift and pin seamline along other side of inset. 4. Fold back so you can stitch on the seamline. Sew from the point out, being careful not to stretch. Note: always maintain grainlines.

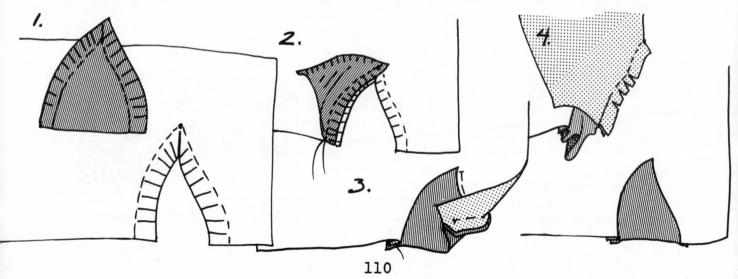

Reversible Patchwork:

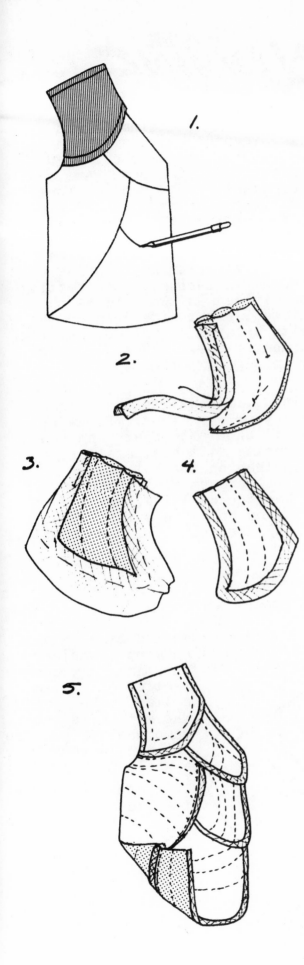

This technique has many plus factors:
...it is reversible with virtually no handwork
...the seams are finished, especially good for unusually shaped pieces
...easy to manage small quilted units and then putting the components together

Method: Choose a fairly simple pattern with 2 or 3 main pattern pieces. Pin any of the straight seams together on the pattern. Trace and cut a paper pattern. Draw a design on the pattern you've just made. To help with the design, think about a stained glass window...the shapes are bias covered. Cut fabric for each shape of the design, adding the seam allowances where the shapes will overlap.

Machine quilt each piece, see page 112. Cut bias strips 3 times the finished width. Stitch a bias to the right side of each piece ¼" from the edge. Turn under and press.

Decisions have to be made as to what pieces will be on the top. The ones that will be underneath will have a bias strip stitched on the 'wrong' side. Turn and press. Now the two shapes will be overlapped, the raw edges will be sandwiched in between the two pieces. Pin and stitch in the ditch...thereby holding both pieces together. Continue until all pieces are connected.

111

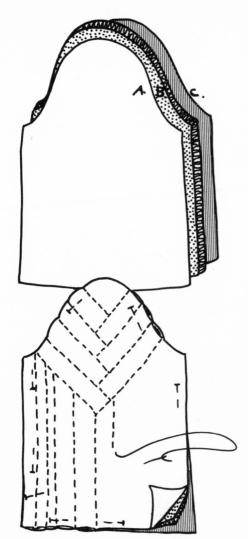

The technique of quilting (putting layers of fabric and batting together with stitching) is a very old procedure. In America, it was used to make quilts. Quilting bees were one of the few social events for women in pioneer times. Other cultures have made padded clothing for warmth, for centuries.

Choose a <u>simple</u> pattern and cut out the garment, the lining and the batting. Choose a thin batting...more flattering. Some batting is fused, can be divided in two. Place the lining to be quilted, right side down on the table. Cover with a layer of cut out batting, top with the garment piece. Baste all three layers together in a grid pattern, 6" to 8" apart.

When hand quilting...if possible use a frame or hoop...to keep your work flat. Be aware of the fact that it should be flat when you finish. Small running stitches, smaller stitch on the top than on the bottom, or a backstitch could be used to fasten the layers together. When machine quilting, use 6 - 8 stitches per inch and hold the material taut as you stitch the lines, so it will be smooth.

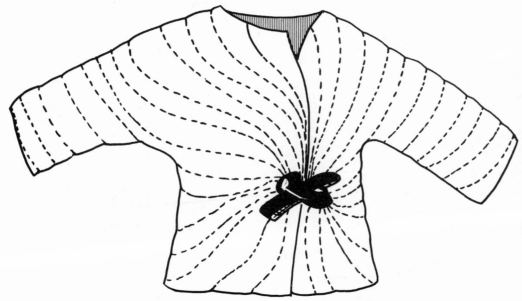

When designing a garment, consider quilting only one section of it...a collar, yoke, cuffs. The method is the same whether you are quilting a pocket or a whole jacket.

The inspiration for the jacket on the left, came from the lines of a woman's hair in a Japanese woodcut. The 'fastener' was actually her hair ornament.

112

Sashiko stitchery is a form of quilting that origi-
nates in Japan. The traditional colors are dark blue
cotton, embroidered with white thread.

Preshrink your fabric. Draw the design you've chosen
on a piece of paper. Trace onto the fabric with the
tracing wheel and carbon. As an alternative method for
applying the design to the fabric, you could make a cardboard template and draw around the shapes with a wash
out sewing pen.

Prepare your fabrics for quilting as on the opposite
page. The stitches are simple running stitches, about
5 - 7 per inch, done as evenly as possible. The stitching is done in a continuous line so plan your stitching
lines efficiently. Also it is important that you leave
the stitches fairly loose so as not to draw up the fabric.

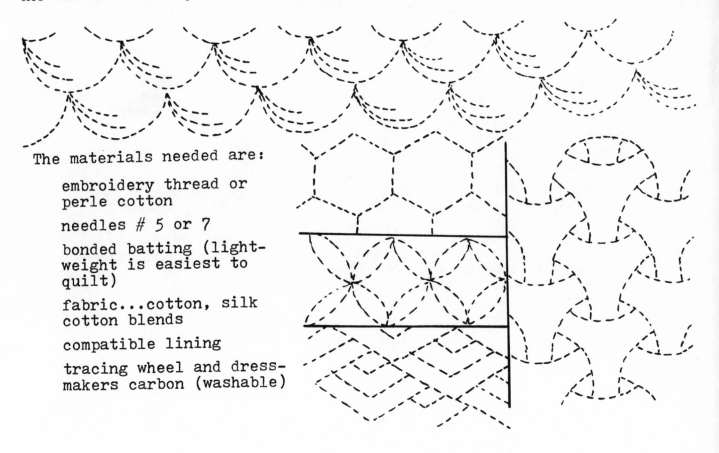

The materials needed are:

    embroidery thread or
    perle cotton

    needles # 5 or 7

    bonded batting (light-
    weight is easiest to
    quilt)

    fabric...cotton, silk
    cotton blends

    compatible lining

    tracing wheel and dress-
    makers carbon (washable)

Trapunto is one form of quilting with a definite embossed effect. The design is stitched and padded so it projects slightly from the background. Draw a simple sketch, see page 7 for contour drawing, or trace the outline of a design you like. Inspirational sources, such as artifacts or oriental metal objects, would be good choices.

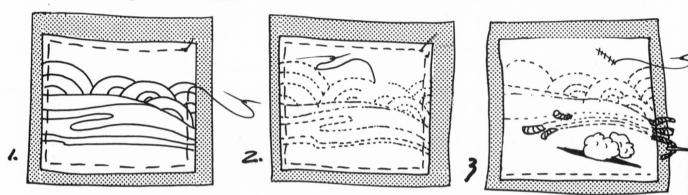

1. Draw the design of your choice on a thin cotton or a knit (there is less puckering if you use a knit). Baste to the wrong side of the fabric to be used for your garment.

2. Machine or hand stitch, thru both layers, on the design lines. Decide what areas are to remain flat and which will be stuffed.

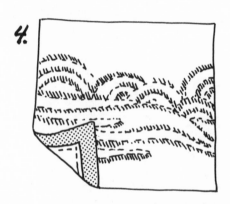

3. From the <u>back</u> cut slits in the lining of the large areas and stuff with polyester batting. Whip the slits together or use fusible interfacing to cover the openings. The small narrow areas are stuffed by using a yarn needle and yarn (acryllic if you intend to wash the garment). Thread yarn needle and pass it thru the backing in those narrow channels...no need to fasten...just leave 1" end and clip.

4. Finished trapunto. A word of caution...don't stuff the shapes too tightly.

The example on the right shows a trapunto piece used on a garment. Although the piece is very small the over all effect is very pleasing.

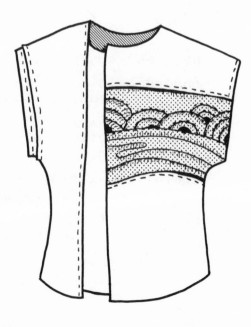

The trapunto technique is one
to consider for sections of
garments. An area that you
would normally quilt, for example...cuffs, shoulder sections, yokes, wide hem bands.
For design ideas refer to
books with line drawings i.e.
stenciling, stained glass pattern books, or even coloring
books.

Materials/Techniques
cross reference

Materials: **Uses:**

BATTING.............................Quilting, Padded Hems, Trapunto

BEADS...............................Covered Buttons, Yarn Beads,
                                    Embroidery, Tassels

BIAS................................Cording, Ties, Buttonloops, Frogs,
                                    Patchwork, Applique, Seam Finishes,
                                    In-seam Pockets, Inset Pockets,
                                    Buttonhole Pockets, Weaving

BRAID...............................Frogs, Tassels, Applique, Weaving,
                                    Trim for Covered Buttons

COINS (with holes in them)........Ties, Beading

CORDING.............................Buttonloops, Buttons, Frogs, Pip-
                                    ing, Padded Hems and Cuffs, Tra-
                                    punto, Wrapping

LEATHER CORDS.....................Frogs, Buttons, Buttonloops,
                                    Weaving

RIBBON..............................In-seam Pockets, Seam Finishes,
                                    Ties, Frogs, Patchwork, Applique,
                                    Weaving, Tassels, Embroidery

TEXTILE TREASURES.................Windows, Applique, In-seam Pockets

YARN OR EMBROIDERY THREAD........Seam Finishes, Seam Joinings, Tra-
                                    punto, Faggoting, Decorative Tacks,
                                    Weaving, Yarn Beads, Smocking, Mir-
                                    ror Embroidery, Tassels, Rope

Bibliography

Bradkin, Cheryl Greider   "The Seminole Patchwork Book"
        Yours Truly Publ. Atlanta   1980
Braun and Schneider   "Historic Costume in Pictures"
        Dover Publ. N.Y.   1975
Brown, Gail   "Sensational Silk"   Palmer & Pletsch
        Portland   1982
Chen, Lydia   "Chinese Knotting"   Echo Publ.   Taiwan 1981
Cho and Grover   "Looking Terrific"   Ballantine Books   N.Y. 1978
Coats & Clark   "101 Embroidery Stitches"   Coats & Clark   N.Y. 1964
De Dillmont, T. "The Complete Encyclopedia of Needlework"
        Running Press, Inc. Philadelphia   1972
Durand, Dianne   "Smocking"   Dover Publ.   N.Y.
Edwards, Betty   "Drawing on the Right Side of the Brain"
        St. Martens Press   N.Y. 1979
Ericson, Lois & Diane   "Ethnic Costume"   Van Nostrand Reinhold
        N.Y.   1979
Erte   "Erte's Fashion Designs"   Dover Publ. N.Y.   1981
Fairservis, Walter A. Jr.   "Costumes of the East"   Chatham Press
        Connecticut   1971
Franck, Frederick   "The Zen of Seeing"   Random House   N.Y.   1973
Hollen, Norma R.   "Pattern Making by the Flat Pattern Method"
        Burgess Publ. Co. Minneapolis   1975
Gostelow, Mary   "The Complete International Book of Embroidery"
        Simon and Schuster   N.Y.   1977
Jackson, Carole   "Color Me Beautiful"   Ballantine Books N.Y. 1981
Matsuya   "Japanese Design Motifs"   Dover Publ. N.Y. 1972
Meilach and Menagh   "Exotic Needlework"   Crown Publ. N.Y. 1978
Nagishkin, Dmitri   "Folktales of the Amur" Harry Abrams Inc.
        N.Y.   1980
Nevelson, Louise   "Dawns and Dusks" Scribner   N.Y.   1976
O'Connor, Kaori   "Creative Dressing"   Routledge & Kegan Paul
        Boston   1980
Ota, Kimi   "Sashiko Quilting"   Kimi Ota, Seattle 1981
Palmer & Pletsch   "Easy, Easier, Easiest Tailoring" Palmer/Pletsch
        Portland   1977
Rex, Chris   "Comfort Clothes"   Celestial Arts   1981
Selbie, Robert   "The Anatomy of Costume"   Crescent Books N.Y. 1977
Sibbett, Ed Jr.   "New Stained Glass Pattern Book" Dover Publ. N.Y.
Snowden, James   "The Folk Dress of Europe"   Mayflower Books
        N.Y.   1979
Stein, W.   "Ancient Ireland" A Coloring Book   Bellerophon Books
        San Francisco   1978
Stuvel, Pieke   "A Touch of Style"   Penguin Books   N.Y. 1981
Tilke, Max   "National Costumes" Hastings House N.Y. 1978
Yarwood, Doreen   "European Costume"   Larousse & Co. N.Y. 1975

Index

About the Authors...

In the past I have taken such titles as wife, mother, student, teacher, weaver, grandparent, author and seamstress. I have retained most of those identities.

No one gives us a title, we have to take one for ourselves. The one I've chosen for this particular segment of my life is designer. I enjoy meeting the challenges and solving the problems that are present in my everyday world.

My life is full...I love it!

Lois

Lois Ericson
P.O. Box 5222
Salem, OR 97304

I'm very involved with understanding and expressing my creative energies. In the past several years that fascination has taken many forms – designing and constructing a passive solar house with my husband Chas, giving birth to our daughter Piper and starting a design business together.

This workbook is the result of a growing and changing bond between my mother and me, the need to share myself as a teacher and a deepening love affair with cloth.

Diane

Diane Ericson
650 Gibson
Pacific Grove, CA 93950

— Workshops available, please write for information —

texture

.......a closer look

Lois Ericson

Texture is usually thought of as something visual, not necessarily
something you can create. This book will give you new insights
into manipulating fabric and fiber in ways you never thought of...
ways of changing a mundane fabric to an extraordinary one. More
than 20 participants will share their expertise in the 224 pages.
200 bl./wh. photos, 16 pages of color. Plastic coated cover,
perfect bound. The retail price is $21.95.

TITLE	PRICE	NO. OF COPIES	TOTAL
TEXTURE...a closer look	$21.95		
FABRICS...RECONSTRUCTED	$13.95		
DESIGN & SEW IT YOURSELF w/Diane Ericson	$14.95		
BELTS...WAISTED SCULPTURE	$11.95		
PRINT IT YOURSELF w/Diane Ericson	$ 6.95		

☐ BILL ME
   WHOLESALE ONLY

☐ PAYMENT ENCLOSED

☐ WORKSHOP INFO REQUEST

☐ WHOLESALE RATES:
   12 OR MORE COPIES
   (YOU CAN MIX TITLES)
   40% DISCOUNT...YOU
   PAY SHIPPING, NET
   30 DAYS. SEND RESALE
   NUMBER.

Add $2.50 P&H - 1 to 3 BOOKS

TOTAL AMOUNT ENCLOSED

MAIL CHECK OR MO TO:
(CANADIAN CUSTOMERS POSTAL MO
ONLY, PLEASE)

Lois Ericson
P.O. Box 5222
Salem, OR 97304

NAME _____

ADDRESS _____

CITY_____ STATE____ ZIP_____

texture

......a closer look

Lois Ericson

Texture is usually thought of as something visual, not necessarily
something you can create. This book will give you new insights
into manipulating fabric and fiber in ways you never thought of...
ways of changing a mundane fabric to an extraordinary one. More
than 20 participants will share their expertise in the 224 pages.
200 bl./wh. photos, 16 pages of color. Plastic coated cover,
perfect bound. The retail price is $21.95.

texture

.......a closer look

Lois Ericson

Texture is usually thought of as something visual, not necessarily something you can create. This book will give you new insights into manipulating fabric and fiber in ways you never thought of... ways of changing a mundane fabric to an extraordinary one. More than 20 participants will share their expertise in the 224 pages. 200 bl./wh. photos, 16 pages of color. Plastic coated cover, perfect bound. The retail price is $21.95.

TITLE	PRICE	NO. OF COPIES	TOTAL
TEXTURE...a closer look	$21.95		
FABRICS...RECONSTRUCTED	$13.95		
DESIGN & SEW IT YOURSELF w/Diane Ericson	$14.95		
BELTS...WAISTED SCULPTURE	$11.95		
PRINT IT YOURSELF w/Diane Ericson	$ 6.95		

Add $2.50 P&H - 1 to 3 BOOKS

TOTAL AMOUNT ENCLOSED

☐ BILL ME
    WHOLESALE ONLY

☐ PAYMENT ENCLOSED

☐ WORKSHOP INFO REQUEST

☐ WHOLESALE RATES:
    12 OR MORE COPIES
    (YOU CAN MIX TITLES)
    40% DISCOUNT...YOU
    PAY SHIPPING, NET
    30 DAYS. SEND RESALE
    NUMBER.

MAIL CHECK OR MO TO:
(CANADIAN CUSTOMERS POSTAL MO
ONLY, PLEASE)

Lois Ericson
P.O. Box 5222
Salem, OR 97304

NAME _____

ADDRESS _____

CITY_____ STATE____ ZIP_____

texture

.......a closer look

Lois Ericson

Texture is usually thought of as something visual, not necessarily something you can create. This book will give you new insights into manipulating fabric and fiber in ways you never thought of... ways of changing a mundane fabric to an extraordinary one. More than 20 participants will share their expertise in the 224 pages. 200 bl./wh. photos, 16 pages of color. Plastic coated cover, perfect bound. The retail price is $21.95.

TITLE	PRICE	NO. OF COPIES	TOTAL
TEXTURE...a closer look	$21.95		
FABRICS...RECONSTRUCTED	$13.95		
DESIGN & SEW IT YOURSELF w/Diane Ericson	$14.95		
BELTS...WAISTED SCULPTURE	$11.95		
PRINT IT YOURSELF w/Diane Ericson	$ 6.95		
Add $2.50 P&H - 1 to 3 BOOKS			
TOTAL AMOUNT ENCLOSED			

☐ BILL ME
   WHOLESALE ONLY

☐ PAYMENT ENCLOSED

☐ WORKSHOP INFO REQUEST

☐ WHOLESALE RATES:
   12 OR MORE COPIES
   (YOU CAN MIX TITLES)
   40% DISCOUNT...YOU
   PAY SHIPPING, NET
   30 DAYS. SEND RESALE
   NUMBER.

MAIL CHECK OR MO TO:
(CANADIAN CUSTOMERS POSTAL MO
ONLY, PLEASE)

Lois Ericson
P.O. Box 5222
Salem, OR 97304

NAME _____

ADDRESS_____

CITY_____ STATE____ ZIP_____